The Marketing Operations Handbook

A Complete Guide to Marketing Operations

Michael McKinnon

The Marketing Operations Handbook

Copyright © 2021 by Michael McKinnon

ISBN: 9798495346598

Disclaimer

Table of Contents

About the Author

Michael McKinnon is the VP of WW Revenue Operations at LogRhythm, a network security firm. With nearly 20 years of experience in operations with companies both large and small, Mike has tackled almost every problem a B2B software organization has encountered. One of Marketo's initial customers back in the early 2000s, Mike began his operations career when marketing technology was exploding, and Marketing departments were searching for ways to prove their worth.

Mike can turn vision into reality through technology, process architecture, and great teamwork. He has a passion for creating high-performing organizations that can track their entire demand engine from lead to bookings. He was most recently featured in Roland Smart's book "The Agile Marketer: Turning Customer Experience into Your Competitive Advantage". He has been a repeat speaker at SXSW, MME, Oracle Open World, and Sirius Decision's Summit on topics ranging from lead nurturing and scoring, to setting up an international demand center.

Acknowledgments

My deepest thanks go to those who helped support me with ideas, motivation, proofreading, and interviews.

I would like to thank my two kids, Jax and Adeline, for their never-ending love and support. Seeing you grow and tackle new challenges with such grace and joy, inspires me to keep growing and learning.

I would also like to thank Michel Ruefenacht and Mike Bernard for their insight and support during COVID. You helped me get started and kept me motivated to finish.

A special thanks to Ashley Kelly for her loving support and her keen eye for editing.

Foreword

Marketing operations rocks.

And, yes, as an advocate and analyst of the blossoming field of marketing technology and operations over the past decade and a half, I'm biased. But it's still an objective truth.

It's rare to have the opportunity to pioneer a whole new profession and to change the dynamics of an entire industry in the process. But that's marketing operations today. And it is transforming the dynamics of the entire marketing industry.

I've often said that there's no better time to be working in marketing. So many innovations. So much power to create experiences on a digital canvas that spans the globe. So much influence and impact on the success of businesses in this new age of the customer. So much opportunity to invent new ways of attracting, engaging, and delighting your audience.

But as exciting as it is to be working in marketing now, it's an even *better* time to be working in marketing operations. Because that's the foundation on which all of these wonderful marketing possibilities are built.

Without excellent marketing operations, there is no marketing anymore.

As a marketing operations leader, you're delivering the capabilities that enable everyone else in marketing to deliver their contributions with maximum efficiency and maximum impact. The work you do is the quintessential multiplier effect.

But what exactly are those capabilities? And how do you implement them?

With such a new field, one that has advanced so quickly in recent years, those answers can be difficult to find. At least they were difficult to find until Michael McKinnon wrote this book.

I have known Mike since 2010. As one of the true pioneers of the field, Michael has been mastering the discipline of marketing operations since back in the early 2000s. He's figured out the processes, the frameworks, the technology, and how they all get synthesized into a high-performance marketing operations machine.

Now, he's taken that hard-won experience and wisdom and put it down on paper for other marketing ops pros — and those who aspire to join their ranks — to accelerate their learning and hone their skills. This book packs a ton of real-world insights and recommendations for practitioners, by a master practitioner.

Wherever you are on your marketing operations journey, this will get you further down the road, faster, and with fewer bumps along the way. From there, you will be well-prepared to discover what's over the next horizon in marketing ops and contribute to the further advancement of this field that you to are helping to pioneer.

I wish you much success and delight.

– Scott Brinker, Editor chiefmartec.com

1
Introduction to Marketing Operations

What is Marketing Operations

If you are reading this book, you may have a pretty good idea about the role marketing operations serves within an organization or you have at least been exposed to the marketing operations concept. During the writing of this book, I interviewed many people and ask them all to define marketing operations. As you can expect, I received varying definitions. Some of the answers focused on the technology, some of them focused on analytics and data, and others execution.

While all the answers were insightful and correct, no one captured the full remit of the modern marketing operations function. A full definition will include all the pieces above as well as several other new disciplines within marketing operations. Below is my attempt at defining marketing operations.

> *Marketing operations operationalizes the marketing organization's strategy, provides analytics to guide decisions, supports and implements the technology roadmap, and proactively plans and manages for growth. Marketing operations also drives efficiencies and greater return into the marketing organization using benchmarking and intelligent process design.*

This is a modern definition of Marketing Operations (MO) that includes all five of the functional areas. However, MO has been around for nearly a hundred years in some form or fashion and has evolved as technology evolves.

History of Marketing Operations

"There is a science to advertising. Experienced advertisers have watched and recorded, tested, and logged, and left records of countless campaigns. In these conditions, advertising and merchandising become a science. Principles are learned and proven by repeated tests."[1]

Written in 1923, it marked the beginning of the accountable marketing mindset. Since that time, the goal has remained the same for marketing operations: report, analyze, and improve. What has changed is the technology that allows us to close the loop between customer interactions and business outcomes.

---

[1] http://www.scientificadvertising.com/ScientificAdvertising.pdf

As you might have noticed, this publication was written around the same time as the Golden Age of Radio was forming, when the medium of commercial broadcast radio grew into the fabric of daily life in the United States, providing news and entertainment to a country struggling with economic depression and war. It is no coincidence that the beginning of marketing operations also coincided with the beginning of mass marketing.

As radio flourished and TV became mainstream, it was apparent that the consumer must be included in marketing strategies. Proctor and Gamble created brand management teams and Harley Proctor was the first advertising and sales manager who created the name, Ivory Soap. By 1960, marketing science institutes started to create surveys that were sponsored by product companies. Consumer product testing was born!

In the 1980s, Computer Identics Corporation (CIC) installed the first true barcode system at General Motors. Later, the National Association of Food Chains developed a Universal Product Code (UPC) for the food industry. Food coupons were the first step in tracking consumer product purchases for marketing purposes and they were a major catalyst in changing marketing strategy.

By the 1990s, because of statistical data and technology, companies had higher expectations. They made their marketing departments responsible and accountable for market research and for ROI. Eventually, customer retention became the next point of focus for marketing. Companies wanted to emphasize the importance of customer loyalty and the competitive edge that it brings. Prompting Peter Drucker to define marketing's goal: "To

3

know and understand the customer so well that the product or service fits him and sells itself."

Innovation came rapidly in the early 2000s because the internet provided a way for marketers to measure inputs and outputs and to rapidly optimize their marketing channels with buyer insights. The book, *The New Marketing Mission*, was published and it proposed "the concept of adding more processing of Metrics Technology to marketing procedures" which is a core tenet of marketing operations. Following the timeline in Figure 1, you can see that from 2005 to 2011 the discipline of marketing operations gained credibility within the industry.

"Engaging digital consumers is not just about spending dollars with Google, Facebook, and Amazon," stated Damian Ryan, a technology, and media M&A partner at BDO who produced the report.

"Global martech spend has leapt again by more than 20 percent in the last year as brands continue to seek a competitive edge and greater efficiencies in the digital economy. To put this into context, martech spend has almost doubled in just two short years in more developed markets such as North America and the UK."

It is important to note that each major transition in marketing has happened alongside a corresponding technology change. In the 1920s, it was radio and TV. Then it was UPCs and RFIDs in the 1980s. In the 2000s, it was the internet and the advent of SaaS that saw the explosion and need for marketing operations. You will see that the major impact the internet had on the MO group is a recurring theme in this book.

The internet gave birth to the SaaS platform which proved to be a boon for marketers who were straddled by IT/IS

4

purchasing considerations. Freed from those considerations, droves of marketing organizations began purchasing technology. According to a Gartner report, CMOs technology spending is said to already outpace that of CIOs.[2] The data-driven efforts of marketing are fueling the increasing need for technology.

In fact, according to the figures in InfotechLead, CMOs in the US alone are expected to invest more than $122 billion in marketing technology and associated services by 2022, up from the estimated $90 billion spent in 2017.[3] The marketing automation market is estimated to contribute $26 billion to that spending within the next three years.[4]

With each new technology, new and deeper buyer insights are opened to the marketer. With those insights, a demand has arisen for new skills in the marketing department—namely, data analysts, technology experts, and process design experts. The stage has been set for the modern MO group which exists in organizations today.

Marketing Operations Today

What is driving the rapid growth in MO function at organizations today? I think there are three critical contributing factors to the rapid growth in marketing operations.

---

[2]https://www.gartner.com/it/content/1871500/1871515/january_3_cmoasbuyingcenter_lmclellan.pdf?userId=83355140http://my.gartner.com/portal/server.pt?open=512&objID=202&mode=2&PageID=5553&ref=webinar-rss&resId=1871515

[3] https://infotechlead.com/cio/cmo-or-cio-who-should-run-marketing-technology-budgets-54430

[4] https://infotechlead.com/cio/cmo-or-cio-who-should-run-marketing-technology-budgets-54430

The first factor is the sheer number of technologies now available to marketers. In May of 2020, Scott Brinker unveiled his latest MarTech count of over 8,000 technologies.

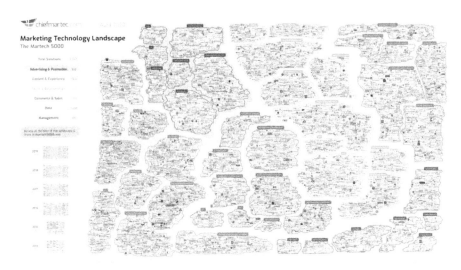

Figure 2 Scott Brinker's 2020 MarTech Stack Graphic https://cdn.chiefmartec.com/wp-content/uploads/2020/04/martech-landscape-2020-martech5000-slide.jpg

This is extraordinary growth from 2011 when he began tracking it. The eight years of MarTech graphics in Figure 3 show the explosion. The number of marketing technologies nearly doubled every year until 2015 and has slowed to a more modest growth of 30–40 percent!

Forrester analysts, Shar VanBoskirk and Drew Green—together with Keith Johnston, Sharyn Leaver, Olivia Morley, and Rachel Birrell—have analyzed the trends in marketing technology. They have stated that the growth of marketing technology spend will outpace that of technology services as marketers emphasize building customer experiences, automating more processes, investing in innovation, and supporting more forms of mobile engagement.[5]

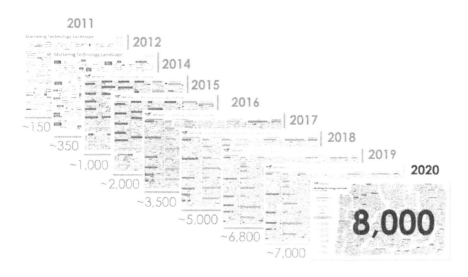

Figure 3 https://cdn.chiefmartec.com/wp-content/uploads/2020/04/martech-landscape-2011-2020.jpg

Technology was no doubt the driving force for my start in marketing operations. The MO group usually begins with trying to manage the ever-growing set of marketing technologies for the marketing organization. Managing technologies, it is quickly realized that accurate reporting can only be had with good data and carefully architected processes. So, what started as a technology remit quickly turns into learning how to operate marketing as a business with revenue accountability, processes, reporting, and the related optimization mindset.

---

[5] https://infotechlead.com/cio/cmo-or-cio-who-should-run-marketing-technology-budgets-54430

The second element is the fact that CMOs are experiencing an enormous amount of pressure to measure ROI from marketing investments. According to the 2019 CMO Survey, the budget spent on marketing analytics has dipped recently but is expected to grow significantly over the next three years to a high of 11 percent. [6]

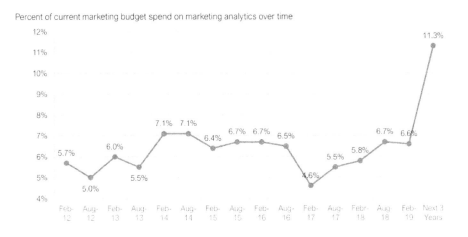

Percent of current marketing budget spend on marketing analytics over time

Figure 4 https://cmosurvey.org/wpcontent/uploads/2019/02/The_CMO_Survey-Highlights and_Insights_Report-Feb-2019-1.pdf p.56

Further, the use of analytics reached the highest point recorded in six years.[7] The drive to prove marketing's value has led CMOs to turn to analytics and big data. Unfortunately, traditionally structured marketing groups do not have that skillset and CMOs have turned to the MO group.

[6] https://cmosurvey.org/wp-content/uploads/2019/02/The_CMO_Survey-Highlights-and_Insights_Report-Feb-2019-1.pdf
[7] https://cmosurvey.org/wp-content/uploads/2019/02/The_CMO_Survey-Highlights-and_Insights_Report-Feb-2019-1.pdf

The third aspect is a byproduct of the internet such as SaaS software. The internet ushered in the "Age of the Consumer" because information about products and services could flow freely among prospects without the need for an organization's narrative. Companies are winning and losing potential customers daily with or without their knowledge.

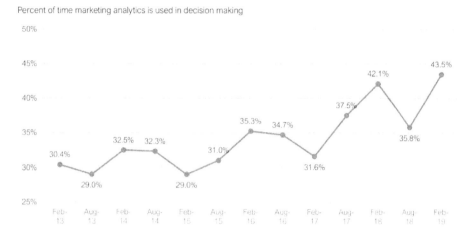

Figure 5 https://cmosurvey.org/wpcontent/uploads/2019/02/The_CMO_Survey-Highlights-and_Insights_Report-Feb-2019-1.pdf p.58

It comes as no surprise that the report, *Rethink the Role of the CMO*, states that CX is the new battleground for brands today.[8] The research finds that nearly 87 percent of organizations agree that traditional experiences are no longer enough to satisfy their customers. The report goes on to state that technology has a key role in delivering a world-class customer experience. Thirty-one percent of organizations have already invested in customer experience technology like AI to help them stay ahead of the

---

[8] https://www.accenture.com/_acnmedia/pdf-87/accenture-rethink-the-role-of-the-cmo.pdf#zoom=50 p5

competition while another 39 percent plan to expand their investment in emerging technology.[9]

The three factors of technology, ROI, and CXM are all pushing marketing operations to the forefront of a marketing organization. What started simply as ownership of technology quickly turned into measuring ROI and driving customer experience because marketing is pressured to do more and more for organizations.

Five Core Functions of Marketing Operations

As stated previously, marketing operations is chartered to operationalize the CMO's strategy, apply analytical insights to drive better decision making, articulate a technology strategy, drive workforce planning initiatives, and proactively plan and manage growth.

Formerly operating as a tactical team focused on activity reporting, tactic planning, and campaign execution, marketing operations is now driving change and supporting growth by informing and enabling marketing strategy and technology. Marketing operations is often relied upon to drive best practices and modern processes into the marketing organization. It is also functioning more and more as a knowledge resource for other parts of a marketing organization, as well.

Today, MO has a large remit within the CMO organization. The five core functions of marketing operations are:

---

9 https://www.accenture.com/_acnmedia/pdf-87/accenture-rethink-the-role-of-the-cmo.pdf#zoom=50 p5

Strategy and Planning

The core function of strategy and planning for marketing operations encompasses budgeting, business planning and interlock, and market analysis. Typically, those activities happen in the fourth quarter as the CMO looks to set the annual plan that encompasses bookings and pipeline targets, campaign calendars, and workforce planning. However, any time new markets or products emerge, strategy and planning become a critical component of go-to-market success.

Marketing operations departments will support the CMO by providing historical data analysis, campaign and tactic effectiveness, and a model for predicting marketing bookings based upon marketing funnel conversions. Ultimately, the MO group should provide the CMO with funnel targets that the marketing organization needs to hit to meet its booking goal.

Technology Management

Technology management is arguably one of the main reasons that marketing operations was formed, as illustrated in the previous chapter. It was certainly the case for me when in 2004 my company, became the 100th customer of Marketo. Within days of purchasing the solution, it became obvious that we did not have the skill set required to effectively run automation software. I had a background in marketing but was residing in technical support. I was moved over to support Marketo and, unwittingly, marketing operations was formed at my company. I would imagine it was a lot like that for most companies in those early days of ravenous technology purchasing by marketing departments.

Mike Bernard, Vice President of Product and Customer Marketing at Optimizely described his marketing operations start similarly. Mike states "Hey, we bought this thing a week ago, figure it out. Those are the instructions I got on day one. I had no background in marketing operations or any of that stuff but through the process of sort of figuring out how to start building email campaigns, how to integrate the data, how to deal with Salesforce, I kind of learned on the job."

Fast forward to the future and marketing operations is now a specialized unit within the marketing organization. MO supports and purchases most of the technology solutions within a marketing organization. They are responsible for vendor management, aligning the technology to the CMO's strategy, and management of the technology.

Support and Administration

A large part of any marketing operations department is supporting their customer, the marketing organization. Often, a ticketing system is used to track the everyday support and administration that the operations department provides to the marketing organization. Ticketing work consists of campaign support and the execution of tactics, reporting, data cleaning, and list loading in addition to all the tasks that must happen at the end of the quarter.

Process Design and Management

In my opinion, this is the most exciting area of marketing operations as it provides incredible business value. A marketing operations department that can design and support complex and efficient processes can provide an immense amount of value to a business. World-class marketing operations departments that excel at this, and understand how process design informs utilization and metrics, are invaluable.

Business Intelligence and Data

This is another exciting area of marketing operations and one that is growing rapidly as new tools emerge that allow organizations to not only collect massive amounts of data but filter through it and act on the pieces that are the most valuable. Let's face it, in most organizations marketing is leading the drive for clean and actionable data that allow them to understand their buyer's journey at increasingly granular levels.

Figure 6 on the next page shows the five functions of the MO group in a table format with their respective subgroups. This book is organized around that structure with each section of the book being about a functional area of the MO group.

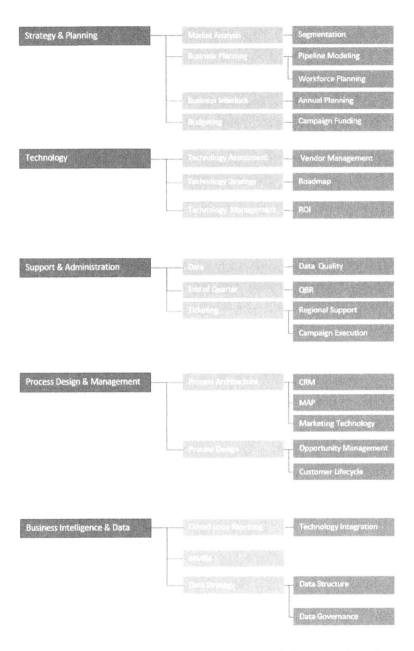

Figure 6 The five functional areas of marketing operations with their respective sub-areas and tactical areas

14

Maturity Modeling

It is important to first understand the maturity of your current MO group in each of the functional areas. Benchmarking your current state is critical to tracking improvement and building a roadmap to maturity. A maturity model, like the one shown on the next page, allows you to assess the maturity of your MO group.

Maturity models are helpful assessments to provide executives and teams with a high-level view of your organization's current state compared to expectations. They are great for revealing areas that are not as mature as expected and areas of strength that can be leveraged. I like using the model because it can provide three great benefits for the operations group:

1. **Roadmap for Improvement**
   The model can provide your group with a roadmap for improvement, outlining each responsibility within each function and describing what it takes to achieve level 5.

2. **Expose the breadth of responsibilities**
   By providing an expansive view of MO responsibilities, the model highlights areas that are not being performed today.

3. **Provide objective comparisons**
   MO groups that perform the same breadth of responsibilities will be able to compare their results across peer groups and organizations.

One final note before using the maturity model is that, depending on company size, some of the functions may never be part of the MO group's remit. For instance, at smaller companies, a lot of the strategy and planning is driven by finance and the sales organization. Keep in mind that it is not necessarily prudent nor feasible to improve in all areas given company size and/or other restrictions your organization may face.

Marketing Operations Maturity Model Index

		Maturity Level	
		Level	Category Score
Strategy and Planning	Market Analysis	1	1.25
	Business Planning	1	
	Business Interlock	1	
	Budgeting	2	
Technology	Vendor Management	4	3
	Technology Strategy	2	
	Technology Management	3	
Support and Administration	Data	1	3
	End of Quarter	1	
	Ticketing	4	
Process Design and Management	Customer Experience	1	2
	Process Architecture	2	
	Process Design	3	
Business Intelligence and Data	Reporting	4	2.25
	Dashboarding	3	
	Data Strategy	1	
	Forecasting	1	
Marketing Operations Maturity Level			2.3

Figure 7 Use the model to map out areas of improvement or areas that are not being performed today.

16

I like to use the Capability Maturity Model Integration (CMMI) framework for software maturity when using the model. In the CMMI framework, maturity levels represent a staged path for an organization's performance and process improvement efforts based on predefined sets of practice areas. Each maturity level builds on the previous maturity levels by adding new functionality or rigor.

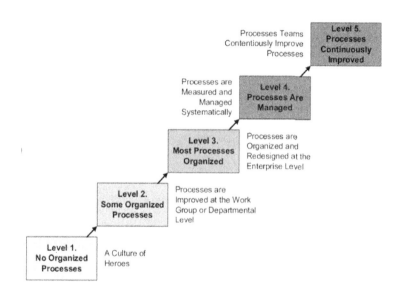

Figure 8 CMMI Framework https://www.researchgate.net/figure/An-Overview-of-the-basic-CMMI-maturity-levels_fig2_319881495

To use the model, begin by assessing the marketing operations function in the five functional areas as outlined earlier in this chapter. You can do that with your MO group or individually with each participant performing the assessment and then bringing the findings together for comparison. Evaluate each topic to see if it meets the level 1 criteria as described above. If it meets the level 1 criteria, move forward to the next level and see if it meets that level's criteria. If only some of the criteria are met, move back to the previous level. Repeat the process for each responsibility within all five functions, first comparing the organization's current state with the description of level 1.

Once the assessment has been completed, you will have a roadmap for improvement that your MO group can follow. You must consider your organization's maturity level in other areas of those functions as well as the maturity level of the MO group. Add a time element, as well, by setting goals such as a move from level 2 to 3 in a year in Strategy and Planning.

Strategy and Planning

Market Analysis estimates implementation of market analysis within MO. As you progress up the levels, marketing analysis is thoroughly conducted before moving into new markets and there is a methodology to do so. The data that is collected for marketing analysis is trusted, accurate, and governed.

Business Planning looks at the implementation of business planning within MO. Progression through the levels relates to the methodology, alignment, and success of the plans.

Business Interlock measures how well MO collaborates with other groups to operationalize marketing's strategy.

Budgeting evaluates the degree to which budgeting is taking place within the MO group.

Technology

Vendor Management evaluates how well MO manages its relationship with the technology vendors including contracts, terms, and fees.

Technology Strategy assesses if the technology aligns with an organization's current goals and allows the organization to scale to support future growth.

Technology Management gauges how well the selected tools are being managed, whether best practices are being followed, and if they are being fully utilized for maximum ROI. Also assessed is the degree to which they are integrated into each other and the rest of the organization.

Support and Administration

Data evaluates whether there is a comprehensive and consistent approach to managing the data with the MAP and/or CRM. Is collection governed? Are inputs validated? How often is data cleansed and appended?

End of the Quarter focuses on how well MO conducts its end-of-quarter activities including attribution, QBR, and data cleanup.

Ticketing assesses how efficiently MO manages its work and whether it can support the needs of the marketing organization. Does the ticketing system allow you to manage resources by providing velocity metrics?

Process Design and Management

Process Architecture gauges how well MO builds processes that support the overall goals of the company.

Process Design evaluates how well MO designs processes that support marketing and interlock with other processes. Also assessed is how well MO aligns its processes with other business units such as sales operations.

Business Intelligence and Data

Closed-Loop Reporting analyzes the reporting maturity of the MO group. As higher levels are reached, MO reporting is used for increasingly strategic objectives, data is trusted, and a single source of truth is established.

MMF looks at how well MO builds effective reporting and dashboarding that is used at all levels of the marketing department to guide decision-making.

Data Strategy evaluates whether there is a comprehensive and consistent approach to managing the data used by marketing and it assesses the alignment of data with other teams.

Forecasting focuses on how well MO forecasts workforce, bookings, pipeline, and various other marketing KPIs.

Common Terms

Before we jump into the main content, I would like to take a moment to clarify some common terms that I often see misused in the industry. As an operations group, creating precise language around business processes and definitions promotes organizational understanding. It also helps to promote the MO group as a trusted and knowledgeable advisor. The two sets of terms I often see misused are 1) bookings and revenue; and 2) contribution and attribution.

Bookings, Billings, and Revenue

In SaaS, three accounting metrics must be understood. There are four if you count deferred revenue which is revenue that is collected but the service has not been provided yet such as in the case of upfront billing.

Bookings

Bookings represent the commitment of a customer to spend money with your company and they are usually tied to a contract at the moment of the signup or subscription. To make it easier, think of the amount as being on the opportunity record. When the opportunity is moved to closed or won, it is the same as the amount on the contract the customer signed.

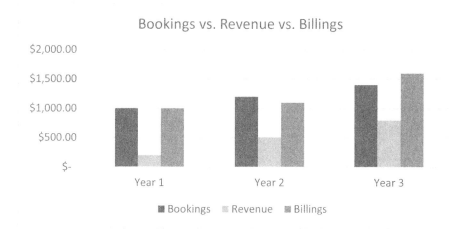

Figure 9 Relationship between bookings, revenue & billings

Revenue

Revenue happens when the service is provided. In the case of a subscription contract, such as SaaS products, the revenue is recognized ratably over the life of the subscription. If you manage things monthly, each month you'll recognize a portion of the money as revenue—and that would be one-twelfth of the total in the case of yearly plans.

Billings

Billings is when you collect your customer's money. It happens at the time of booking if they're paying you months in advance, or at the time of revenue recognition if they're paying you monthly - even if they are committed to a full year.

Contribution and Attribution

These two terms are commonly interchanged but, when examined closely, should refer to two different methodologies within your marketing organization.

I spoke about this with David Lewis on his podcast, DemandGen Radio in January 2021.[10] It is important to understand the distinction between contribution and attribution and to communicate that to the appropriate stakeholders.

Contribution

The process of allocating revenue back to the marketing department through a structured and agreed-upon process. Marketing contribution to bookings is often the main KPI of a marketing organization and can be split into two types:

1. **Sourced:** Sourced bookings are opportunities that can be identified as having originated from marketing activities. If the telequalificaiton group is within marketing, the generation of an opportunity from a TQL is often the indicator of marketing sourced. If marketing is making

---

[10] http://demandgenradio.com/mobile/e/202-how-to-prove-marketing-s-impact-using-attribution-ft-michael-mckinnon/

the handoff to sales at MQL, then an opportunity created from an MQL will typically indicate marketing sourced.

2. **Influenced:** Influenced is often defined as a marketing touch on an individual who is associated with an opportunity.

Both influenced and sourced can be defined in several ways within an organization. The sales group must be involved in the definition so they understand how the data will be captured and analyzed. Transparency is key here if you want the organization to buy into marketing's contribution.

Attribution

The process of allocating revenue back to marketing activities so the organization understands their effectiveness and allocates the budget properly. Accurate attribution at all levels of marketing activities is only possible with a campaign architecture that supports the marketing organization's go-to-market strategy. The section entitled Campaign Funding and Planning in the next chapter goes over campaign architecture in detail.

While a full discussion of marketing attribution is beyond the scope of this book, it is helpful to know there are several attribution models. The next page shows the most common models that help you understand the effectiveness of different marketing activities at different points in the funnel.

First Touch Attribution

Last Touch Attribution

Lead Creation Attribution

Equal Touch Attribution

Opportunity Creation Attribution

Custom (Z, W, U) Touch Attribution

Figure 10 Six of the most common attribution models

For a more detailed look at those models, you can listen to my talk at the MarTech 2020 conference.[11]

11 https://events.martechconf.com/virtual-fall-2020/edit-149?i=VqN2RUU366OeUubbfds3lRtJV9wZLNwZ

2
Strategy and Planning

In Strategy and Planning (S&P), marketing operations partners with the CMO to operationalize the marketing strategy. Critically, it is the area where marketing operations can highlight marketing's value to the organization. A strong marketing operations department will have massive amounts of data to analyze from the various technologies they support, allowing them to provide deep and actionable insights to the CMO and the rest of the business.

The S&P process will provide the foundation for the CMO's go-to-market strategy by aligning budgets, resources, and market analysis. At its highest level, MO will ensure interlock between the go-to-market strategy and the booking goal of marketing with the rest of the organization.

During my career in the early 2000s, marketing departments were buying technology to understand their buyer's journey at ever-deepening levels.

In 2005, we had Marketo, and Salesforce.com to help with strategy and planning.

We analyzed opportunity conversion data in SFDC and Marketo's top of the funnel metrics to budget the number of MQLs needed to hit our booking goals.

It was our second year of Marketo ownership and the technology had already pushed our group into the strategy and planning area of marketing operations. As I mentioned in the maturity model, no journey is linear and mine was no different.

S&P facilitates the CMO's coordination with the sales, product, and corporate functions to ensure alignment on business objectives. It also coordinates regular business reviews of plan progress.

Ultimately, S&P communicates who is responsible for what and outlines how and when something will get done. It also aligns funding to ensure success and establishes what the expected result will be and how it will be measured.

S&P encompasses four functional areas which then inform five subfunctions that help to align the marketing function with other business functions.

Market Analysis

Market analysis and segmentation are the core of S&P. The function and its corresponding sub-functions allow an organization to make informed decisions about which markets they would like to enter or exit, how big those markets are, and what types of resources they should allocate to those markets given their organization's booking goal. It can also help an organization make future product decisions and give a forward-looking view on the attractiveness of current markets.

There are three ways to determine a market's sizing. An organization's product set, maturity level, and revenue goals will help determine which methodology to use.

The most common method is Total Addressable Market (TAM). Most organizations use this method because the data that supports it is most easily obtained via B2B databases like ZoomInfo or Hoovers. The TAM simply assesses the size of a market by the number of accounts regardless of the organization's ability to capture that demand based on its service or product offerings. TAM is often used for long-term planning purposes such as projecting the maximum possible revenue of a proposed new product or the potential value of entering a specific geographic market. Calculating TAM by value is another helpful way to understand the total revenue potential in a market. It is a relatively simple calculation that multiplies the number of units or accounts by the known or anticipated average selling price (ASP). TAM is the most rudimentary of all three market-sizing methodologies, but it is better than no sizing!

The second method, and lesser-known, is Total Serviceable Market (TSM) which is the portion of the TAM that can be reached given the offerings of the organization. TSM is calculated by understanding that not every account within a TAM will need your offering. TSM adds a layer of realism to the TAM and gives a much more realistic projection of future revenue potential within a given market. An example of TSM calculation for a ten-person company that sells accounting software to businesses under 500 employees would be different than a thousand-person company with wholesale relationships. In both instances, the TAM is the same. They are all organizations that need account software but, for the larger company, its serviceable market is much larger due to its extended reach through their wholesale channels.

The last type of market sizing, Total Obtainable Market (TOM), is the most confining and is the most accurate when it comes to predicting the number of customers your organization can capture in the near term. TOM further slices the TSM by adding a layer of feasibility to the analysis including given competitors, existing wallet share, and your organization's offering features and functions. To continue the earlier example of the accounting software business, if three-year contracts were standard, the TOM would slice the TSM further to the accounts that had contracts expiring in the current year. Or, if an offering was missing a feature such as vertical needs, the TOM would eliminate those accounts.

Once the appropriate market sizing methodology has been confirmed, you must identify the segments within that market. Again, the exercise is a narrowing of focus to understand the total market (using whichever model you decided on) and what segments in the market need to be addressed individually because they have different buying needs, industries, or geographical differences. Table 1 illustrates the process of segmentation by showing the relationship between markets and segments using the example of accounting software.

Equally important in the segmentation process is to understand the unit to be counted within each segment. In the diagram above, companies or accounts are the units to be counted. In some situations, for instance in hospitals, a common unit is the number of beds. In other instances, the buyer is the unit to be counted. In the accounting software example, the head of accounting might be the unit counted. In any case, the unit is important to understand because it drives the next phase of business planning.

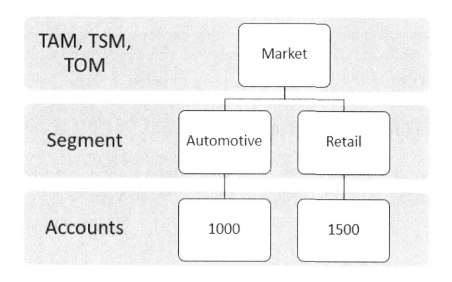

Table 1 The relationship between TAM, Segments, and Accounts

Business Planning

While market analysis is often considered a component of business planning, and rightly so, for this book I have broken out business planning into two components: booking and pipeline modeling (which includes waterfall modeling) and workforce modeling. The two common methods of business planning that are most familiar are called bottom-up or top-down. A bottom-up plan often starts with the marketing booking goal or contribution percent and works toward the pipeline and funnel goals. A top-down plan often starts with the marketing organization being

29

given a budget and then they work toward their booking goal. Both methods are common, depending on many internal factors within the company, but I believe a more precise approach is a bottom-up plan. You should prepare a bottom-up forecast before you get a budget pushed on you or you are in danger of your plan not reflecting accurate selling and market conditions. Since you know when your company planning happens, it behooves you to be ready with the appropriate data to ensure you can conduct a proper bottom-up analysis.

Booking and Pipeline Modeling

Booking and pipeline modeling allows you to accurately predict the bookings your marketing department can contribute and the necessary pipeline to achieve the bookings.

Let's walk through a basic example of this bottom-up analysis in the steps below:

1. **Booking Goals:** The booking goal is the total goal for the entire organization. That can be given to you by the board of directors, the CEO, or any number of other people.

2. **Quota Goal:** The booking goal must be converted into a quota goal before marketing can calculate their contribution. Quotas are determined by over-assigning or uplifting the company's booking goal with an understanding that you will have sales reps who overperform, underperform, or who are ramping up because they are new hires. Typically, that is called attainment or, in other words, the amount each rep will attain on their quota. Quota gives the company padding against their goal.

You can calculate historical attainment by looking at the performance of reps against goal over time or you can use the standard of 20 percent over-assignment. You can also simply divide the booking goals by .8:

Booking Goal ÷ .8.

3. **Marketing's Contribution:** From the total quota goal, you must figure out marketing's contribution by calculating a three-year historical average of marketing's contribution. Using the average as a baseline, you can adjust with the understanding that any large deviation from the average can be an area of concern.

   The table below shows an example of a marketing organization's three-year contribution:

Year 1	Year 2	Year 3
18%	20%	22%

Figure 1 Three-year contribution

Once you know the three-year average, you can calculate marketing's contribution using the three-year average as a start

Total Bookings	*$96M*
Total Quota	$120M
Marketing's Contribution (three-year avg.)	20%
Marketing's Booking Goal	$24M

Figure 2 Calculating marketing's booking goal as a percent of company booking goal

4. **Pipeline to Quota Ratio:** The pipeline to quota ratio or coverage can be determined by looking at a company's historical win rate or coverage ratio. Coverage is the inverse of the win rate. A win rate of 20 percent indicates a needed coverage ratio of 5x. The less coverage a company needs, the more efficient they are at converting pipeline to bookings.

5. **Total Pipeline:** Total pipeline can be calculated by multiplying the marketing contribution by the coverage rate:

Total Bookings	*$96M*
Total Quota	$120M
Marketing's Contribution (three-year avg.)	20%
Marketing's Booking Goal	$24M
Total Marketing Pipeline (5x)	$120M

Figure 3 Calculating marketing's booking goal as a percent of company booking goal

6. **Existing Pipeline:** Every year opportunities created in the previous year carry over into the new year. Depending on your company's sales cycle, that could be a sizeable amount. You must calculate the carryover to understand the amount of net new pipe that must be created in the new year. An important step is an analysis of the carried-over opportunities to make sure they are viable.

Total Bookings	$96M
Total Quota	$120M
Marketing's Contribution (three-year avg.)	20%
Marketing's Booking Goal	$24M
Total Marketing Pipeline (5x)	$120M
Carry over Pipe	$20M

Figure 3a Calculating marketing's booking goal as a percent of company booking goal

7. **Net New Pipeline:** Once the carryover pipe has been calculated, you can arrive at the total net new pipe by subtracting:

Total Bookings	$96M
Total Quota	$120M
Marketing's Contribution (three-year avg.)	20%
Marketing's Booking Goal	$24M
Total Marketing Pipeline (5x)	$120M
Carry over Pipe	$20M
Total Net New Pipe	$100M

Figure 3b Calculating marketing's booking goals as a percent of company booking goals

You have now defined marketing's contribution in terms of pipe and bookings. The next step is to bring the numbers into your waterfall model so you can translate them into lead goals for

33

your demand generation teams, SDR/BDR teams, and to align your sales organization on deliverables.

Waterfall Modeling

Waterfall modeling is the process of determining lead goals for your marketing organization so they can properly plan their budget, workforce, and marketing strategy. The four components of waterfall modeling are:

1. **Average Selling Price (ASP):** This is the average selling price of a booking. To calculate ASP, divide the total value of won bookings by the number of won bookings:

$$Total\ \$\ of\ Bookings \div Total\ \#\ of\ Bookings = ASP$$

2. **Cost Per Inquiry (CPI):** The cost per inquiry is one of the foundational budgetary items for marketing. An inquiry is most commonly defined as a form fill but can often take the form of a booth scan, booth visit, or inbound phone call. The purpose of marketing campaigns is to generate inquiries that are developed into MQLs. As you will learn later, each marketing tactic can have its own cost per inquiry but, for waterfall modeling, you should use a CPI that covers all tactics. If your budget is in separate regions like APAC, EMEA, or LATAM, you should calculate a CPI for each region:

$$Total\ Program^{12}\ Budget \div Total\ \#\ of\ Inquiries = Cost\ Per\ Inquiry$$

---

[12] Program dollars are the budgetary spend that is directly related to demand generation efforts. This is often limited to tactical marketing spend such as webinars, PPC, content syndication, display, events, etc. PR/AR/IR are usually excluded from this spend.

3. **Conversion Rates:** You must also know the conversion rates through your waterfall. Deals will travel most commonly from Inquiry to MQL to TQL and then are accepted by your sales team and sales are qualified into opportunities.

4. **Velocity:** Velocity is the time it takes in days to travel between the stages of your waterfall. The most common way to do that is to timestamp your arrivals into each stage of the waterfall. Of the four components, velocity is the least important as it times the arrivals in each stage but does not affect the overall number. It is also the hardest to track without proper stage governance.

With the four components of waterfall modeling known, you can plan your lead waterfall and give an accurate prediction of the quantity needed at each stage. In Figure 4, we tie together our bookings, pipeline, and waterfall model to properly plan marketing's KPIs for the year.

Marketing's Booking Goal	$24,000,000
ASP	$120,000
Cost Per Inquiry	$10
Conversion and Velocity	Conversion (%)
INQ to MQL	34%
MQL to TAL	95%
TAL to TQL	10%
TQL to SAL	94%
SAL to SQL	65%
SQL to Closed Won	20%
Full Conversion Rate	0.4%
Inquires Per Deal	253
Inquiries Needed	50,670
Number of Won	200
Budget Needed	$506,700

Figure 4 Completing the waterfall to arrive at budget needed

With the total number of inquiries known, you can complete the rest of the required waterfall model and arrive at a quantity per stage based on your conversion. You can take it a step further and use velocity to calculate the month of arrivals at each stage but for the example below I will just use the conversion rates.

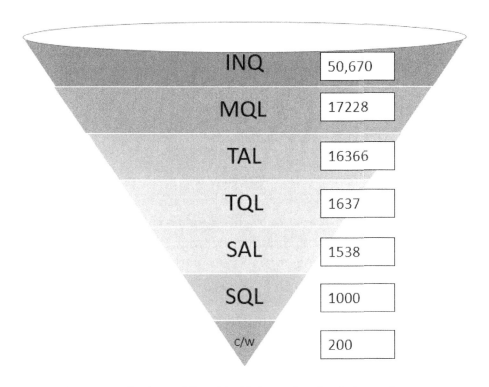

Figure 5 Completed waterfall model with the number of arrivals at each stage

Workforce Modeling

Having completed our booking goal and waterfall modeling, we can start allocating the appropriate resources to ensure the marketing organization can achieve its plan. Workforce modeling will also help you to recognize any gaps in skills that may need to be added in the upcoming year so that you can plan those hires with Finance. It stands to reason you have most of these skills in your organization and you may be able to hire from within.

The table below represents companies of varying revenue sizes and the varying levels of marketing operations maturity they may require. It is written with an understanding that larger companies will have different operational needs than smaller companies. Also, it is important to know that some functions will be moved into other departments, depending on the size of a company.

I split companies into the following revenue bands:

1. $0–100M:
   - ➢ Companies of this size might have just purchased a CRM tool like Salesforce.com with ownership usually residing within Sales or IT/IS. At the higher end of this band, they might also be considering a marketing automation platform (MAP). Staffing in marketing operations might be nonexistent or a shared responsibility within marketing.

2. $101M–$500M:
   - ➢ A MAP service is usually required at this stage and process interlock between departments becomes more important as marketing starts to do more to drive growth. There are now often multiple sources of data coming from web analytics, MAP, CRM platforms, and various other vendors that are being used. Marketing planning and budgeting start to become important as well.

3. $501M–$1B:
   - ➢ Companies in this band usually have multiple product sets and have expanded into international territories which require in-region marketing operations personnel and a tighter focus on departmental alignment. Data quality, if not an earlier focus, now becomes a large issue as multiple databases exist, and one view of the truth is hard to establish.

4. $1.1B–$5B:
   - ➢ Data quality becomes an even larger problem at this level as most likely there have been acquisitions and the acquisitions come with databases that must be integrated into the parent company. At this stage, you will have regional operations groups that used shared services and ticketing to complete the amount of work being generated by the field and senior staffing. If a demand center was not established at the earlier stage, it will be at this stage to ensure operational efficiency and reporting alignment.

5. $5B+:
   - ➢ At this level, marketing operations is the centralized role for all reporting, process, data management, and budgeting for the entire marketing organization. A massive amount of marketing technology is being supported around the globe and operations must work closely with multiple field teams to ensure campaigns are being run consistently in each region. The leader of the marketing operations team is often considered the CIO of marketing at this level.

As you can see, as a company grows, more emphasis is placed on data management and planning as those functions are taken directly on by the marketing organization from other departments such as Finance and IS/IT. Reporting demands increase as well as field teams, senior-level, and other departments begin to request reports from the various technologies that marketing supports. Systems management and process management, usually well-defined at this point, start to play a lesser role.

Business Interlock

Business interlock is more than just simply letting other departments know what you are doing. It is one of the most important things a marketing department can do to ensure other departments within the organization are aware of marketing's contribution to the company and the methodology of the contribution calculation.

Business interlock allows departments to align their strategies under the corporate strategy. It also allows you to understand departmental focus for the upcoming year so dependencies can be identified.

In the past fifteen years since the advent of SaaS, marketing has fought to change its reputation as an expense center to that of a revenue generator. Unfortunately, in some companies, senior staffing still looks at marketing as an expense. The more communication marketing can do, the better they can position themselves as a growth engine for new markets and opportunities.

If you do not conduct business interlock as part of your yearly planning, you run the risk of other departments, especially sales, not being aligned to your goals. One of the easiest ways to do that is to add a sourcing matrix to your yearly planning methodology and to invite other departments into your planning process. Here below is the table presented in pipeline modeling:

Total Bookings	$96M
Total Quota	$120M
Marketing's Contribution (three-year avg.)	20%
Total Marketing Contribution	$24M
Total Marketing Pipeline (5x)	$120M
Carryover Pipe	$20M
Total Net New Pipe	$100M

Figure 6 Example Pipeline Model

You can see that this outlines only marketing contribution and methodology. Typically, an organization can have three sources upon which it can draw revenue: channel, direct sales (Field sales and CSMs), or marketing. Understanding the historical contributions of those three sources can help you achieve understanding from your revenue-generating partners. A great way to do that is to create a sourcing matrix built on three-year trend data (Figure 7) which allows each group to see their contribution.

Figure 7 shows the three-year trending by source and uses the trend to calculate the contribution of each source on a quota goal of $120M. The table should be used when conducting yearly planning with representatives from sales, channel, and marketing present. The percent goal column can be adjusted to change the dollar goal.

In Thousands	Type	Y2	%	Y3	%	3 yr.	Goal	$ Goal
Marketing	New	17,600	22.0%	18,000	20%	20%	20%	24,000
Channel	New	8,000	10%	9,000	10%	10%	10%	12,000
	Existing	12,000	15.0%	13,500	15%	15%	15%	18,000
Direct Sales	New	25,600	32%	27,000	30%	30%	30%	36,000
	Existing	20,000	25.0%	22,500	25%	25%	25%	30,000
		80,000		90,000	100%	100%	100%	120,000

Figure 7 Three-year trending by source

The outcome is to have everyone agree upon the percentage contribution that will come from each source. Inevitably, there will be some back and forth on percent but ultimately the goal should be to have all parties agree so plans can be solidified for the upcoming year.

Michel Ruefenacht, Chief Marketing Officer at YesWeHack, describes the results of poor business interlock between sales and marketing.

His business was growing, and they had expanded their products offering (through an acquisition). They hired more salespeople, had to rework their account coverage, and introduced a new account segmentation based on size, wallet-share and potential. These changes created new account "buckets" and they had to change the go-to-market strategy to best serve these segmented accounts.

Marketing management instructed field marketing to work closely with the sales peers to adapt their marketing programs to align with the new GTM strategy. A few weeks later all plans (captured in marketing decks) were aligned with the new segmentation.

Michel states "I was keeping track of all the detailed plans and tactics in our monster excel spreadsheet and I wondered, how come the activities didn't change? The same old activities got renamed and re-aligned to the new segmentation, with the same old tactics. It didn't take too long to realize that Marketing was continuing to generate demand in market segments and accounts that were not a high priority (or high propensity to buy). Most demand was still created in the lower end of the market, a segment that was already covered by our partners through co-op funding. When we investigated the root cause, we found out that field marketing was trying to please their sales counterpart by continuing to invest in the same activities (mainly events)."

Two main takeaways for Michel are more upfront alignment between the departments so the strategy is aligned down to the field, and don't assume that things have changed because a PowerPoint deck says so. Measure what you expect and use data to have factual conversations.

Budgeting

Once marketing knows their waterfall and booking goals, the CMO will need help in understanding where to allocate program dollars to maximize spending and achieve their goals. The budgeting process will help the CMO and the demand generation managers understand the most efficient mix of marketing tactics based upon budget allocation.

The budgeting section is split into two main sections. The first section will take a look at how marketing budgets are typically arrived at and it shows an example budget. The second section illustrates how MO can help demand generation managers optimize their spending within their allocated budget. However, allocating budget at a tactical level requires a tightly governed campaign structure that tracks spending down to that level. The section will also give an example of such a campaign structure.

Marketing Budgets

First, let's look at the mechanism for funding marketing organizations. Most companies try to keep marketing expenditures within a certain percentage of overall revenue. The chart below shows funding as a percent of revenue for different size organizations.

	<$100M	$100M–$500M	$501M–$1B	$1.01B–$5B	>$5B
Low	8%	5%	4%	3%	2%
Mid	12%	8%	6%	6%	5%
High	16%	12%	8%	8%	7%

Figure 8 Approximate marketing budgets as % of revenue

You can see that a low-funded marketing department in a company generating $500M should expect about $25,000,000 in budget. However, a high-funded department could see around $60,000,000 in budget. It depends on the company's strategy for growth versus profit and other various market factors.

Typically, a marketing department will have about a 55 percent/45 percent split between personnel and demand generation/programs. There are many benchmarks on the percentage of marketing spend available online. They can give a good idea of how much other organizations are spending in certain areas.

Understanding how the total budget can be allocated is important and it is helpful to show how it all ties together as seen in Diagram 9. Let's continue with our example from above and assume we are a mid-funded organization with revenue between $100M and $500M which gives us a total marketing budget of $8M on our bookings target of $100M.

Figure 9 illustrates how it all ties together. We can use the diagram to guide our discussion through the individual parts.

Total marketing budget can be split into two main categories: Personnel/Systems/CapEx and Demand Generation or Program Spend.

1. **Personnel** represents the people and systems-based costs and, due to the nature of technology contracts, is the least flexible portion of the budget. This includes compensation, benefits, training, and travel. The systems-based portion of this budget is usually bound by vendor contracts and, therefore, is the easiest to predict year-over-year.

2. **Demand Generation** constitutes all spending that is for the development and execution of your initiatives. It also includes shared services, agency work, corporate communications, and the website.

Figure 9 illustrates the relationship between budgeting and campaign execution. Marketing operations is a critical stakeholder in both budget allocation and campaign execution.

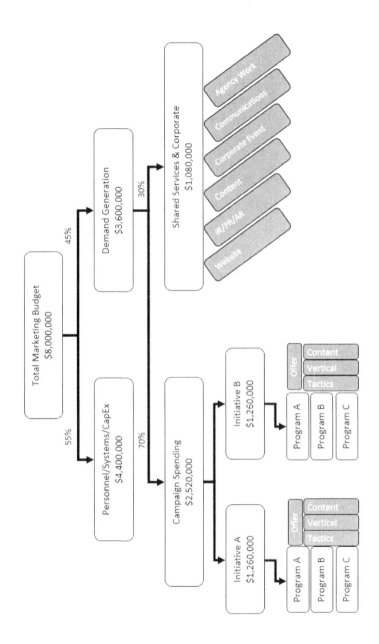

Figure 9 Example of a marketing budget

46

Campaign Funding and Planning

Campaign planning typically resides in the domain of the CMO and the demand generation team. The planning conducted by that group will encompass messaging, markets, design, trade shows, and a whole host of other items that will help the organization achieve its booking goals. MO must be part of that planning conversation so they will understand the reporting needs and be able to build the appropriate architecture to support the demand generation team.

The proper architecture is critical if the demand generation teams and marketing leaders want to understand how various tactics and messages are performing. It is helpful for MO to provide a template to the demand generation team so they can start thinking about their reporting needs at various levels.

Figure 10 is an example hierarchy of how all the channels, tactics, and activities relate to one another. It is helpful to first define some of the terms that will be used in the hierarchy, so everyone is using the same vocabulary. For instance, the word campaign can have many different definitions.

You can substitute any terms for the ones I use. The important thing is that your marketing organization agrees with them. You will notice that I do not use the word, campaign, in any of these definitions. That is done on purpose as you will see later when we discuss execution.

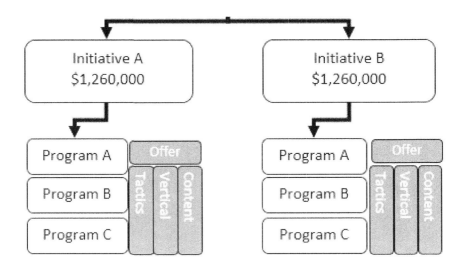

Figure 10 Example of a campaign hierarchy

Initiative

An Initiative is the highest-level roll-up of programs and activities. It is at least twelve months in duration and is focused on a buyer's need and not products that are being sold. It contains the components that are used to achieve the objective. An initiative also contains a high-level message that can be cascaded down into the programs that are contained within it.

Program

A program is the second level and inherits the Initiative's core message but with distinct differences that fit the program's objectives. I have been at companies where the programs are verticals, products, or geographies. Programs carry with them specific objectives that, if achieved, contribute to the Initiative's objective.

Activity

The activity level contains the offer which is more commonly referred to as the call to action. There are four basic types of activities: content promotions with various tactics, webinars, events, and Inbound promotions.[13] An activity has a specific piece of content attached to it and can also target various verticals as well.

Tactic

The tactic communicates the offer within the activity. It is the promotional channel of the offer. This is the lowest level in the hierarchy and is what most people call a campaign. There is a myriad of tactics at the disposal of a demand generation manager.

Tactics	PPC
	Direct Mail
	Display Advertising
	LinkedIn
	Facebook
	Twitter
	Email
	SEO

---

[13] Inbound promotions include free trials, live demos, request demo, and request more information—the whole range of inbound calls to action.

The main purpose of the tactic is to drive traffic to the landing page and get prospects to fill out the offer form.

With the definitions clear, the operations team will be able to build out the hierarchy and reporting structure within their marketing systems which usually consist of a MAP and CRM. For simplicity's sake, let's take Initiative A and flip it horizontally for a clearer picture of the proposed architecture within the systems.

Using the campaign object in your CRM or some equivalent in your MAP, you can align each level to that object and then join the objects in a parent-child hierarchy. UTM codes and/or referrer IDs are usually reserved for the tactics. You can calculate the total cost and understand ROI at each level if you capture the costs on the campaign record in your CRM.

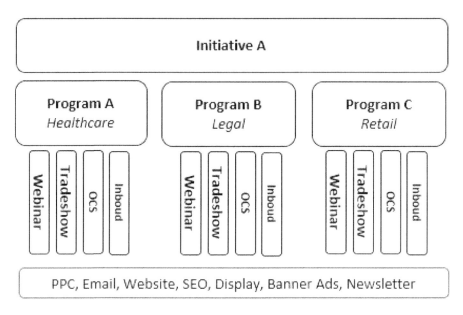

Figure 11 Campaign hierarchy in detail

With the architecture established, we can assign our objectives at each level. Let's look at the diagram again with the objectives visible.

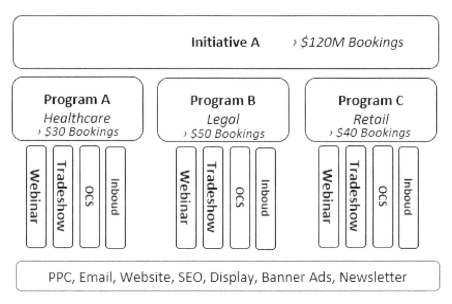

Figure 12 Campaign hierarchy in detail with booking goals

The next step is to use lead modeling to calculate the amount of budget you will apply to each tactic (and program) to reach your booking goal.

Lead Flow Modeling

Lead modeling is used to predict future performance based on the historical performance of your activities and tactics. The lead model allows budgeting to support your booking goal. It also gives the demand generation team a set of waterfall goals by activity that they can monitor to see if they are on target.

The lead model on the next page allows the demand generation team to adjust spending per activity and see the impact on their lead goals based on the cost and historical conversion of those tactics

Let's go through the five areas of the model and see how they can guide your demand generation teams. Sections 1 and 2 are outputs and are not able to be manipulated.

1. The top section is outputs based upon the inputs in sections three, four, and five. The goal columns are the goals pulled from the lead model. The projected columns are the projections based upon the inputs. The percent in projection to goal is the percent to goal based on your inputs.

2. This section breaks down the offer types and shows the waterfall projections based on the variables you manipulate in blue.

Sections 3, 4, and 5 are inputs that the demand generation team can manipulate to change their outputs in Sections 1 and 2.

3. You can change your spending in each of the offer types and move money around between quarters and offers.

4. You can change the cost per inquiry if desired. The current numbers are the historical cost per inquiry but, if your demand generation team wanted to project a lower cost of inquiry from an offer type, they can do that there.

5. This section shows the historical waterfall conversion rates by the offer. The 2020 goal row shows the conversion rates that were input into the annual planning model that was completed in previous

sections. That allows the team to understand that their budget was given to them with certain performance assumptions and, if they fall below those conversion assumptions, their budget will fall short in generating the necessary inquiries.

Once the lead flow model is completed, you can now apply waterfall goals to each activity for the demand generation team. You can update the campaign template with the necessary goals and build dashboards. Figure 15 shows the updated campaign template.

% to Quota Goal

TOTAL	Q1 2020 Goal	Projected	% Projection to Goal	Q2 2020 Goal	Projected	% Projection to Goal	Q3 2020 Goal	Projected	% Projection to Goal	Q4 2020 Goal	Projected	% Projection to Goal
Inquiry	12,841	11,998	93%	12,841	10,750	84%	12,841	12,287	96%	12,841	9,654	75%
MQLs	4,366	3,602	83%	4,366	3,133	72%	4,366	3,592	82%	4,366	3,045	70%
TQLs	478	339	71%	478	316	66%	478	337	71%	478	315	66%
SALs	463	331	72%	463	309	67%	463	330	71%	463	309	67%
SQLs	300	182	61%	300	170	57%	300	181	60%	300	170	57%

		Q1 2020	Q2 2020	Q3 2020	Q4 2020
ORGANIC	Inquiry	1,626	1,626	1,626	1,626
	MQLs	688	688	688	688
	TQLs	51	51	51	51
	SALs	50	50	50	50
	SQLs	28	28	28	28
INBOUND	Inquiry	356	356	356	356
	MQLs	280	280	280	280
	TQLs	178	178	178	178
	SALs	175	175	175	175
	SQLs	96	96	96	96
PPC	Inquiry	755	503	508	755
	MQLs	519	346	350	519
	TQLs	27	18	18	27
	SALs	26	17	18	26
	SQLs	14	10	10	14
OCS	Inquiry	2,678	2,678	2,678	1,785
	MQLs	377	377	377	251
	TQLs	9	9	9	6
	SALs	9	9	9	6
	SQLs	5	5	5	3
EVENT	Inquiry	5,003	4,007	5,539	3,553
	MQLs	1489	1193	1649	1057
	TQLs	69	56	77	49
	SALs	66	53	74	47
	SQLs	37	29	40	26
WEBINAR	Inquiry	1,580	1,580	1,580	1,580
	MQLs	249	249	249	249
	TQLs	4	4	4	4
	SALs	4	4	4	4
	SQLs	2	2	2	2

VARIABLE BUDGET
Change budget to alter the projected lead volume

Type	Q1-FY20	Q2-FY20	Q3-FY20	Q4-FY20
Organic	$ -	$ -	$ -	$ -
Inbound	$ -	$ -	$ -	$ -
PPC	$ 150,000	$ 100,000	$ 101,000	$ 150,000
OCS	$ 150,000	$ 150,000	$ 150,000	$ 100,000
Event	$ 374,614	$ 300,000	$ 414,714	$ 266,000
Webinars	$ 100,000	$ 100,000	$ 100,000	$ 100,000
Lead Gen*	$ -	$ -	$ -	$ -
Grand Total	$ 774,614	$ 650,000	$ 765,714	$ 616,000

COST PER INQUIRY: Historical Cost per Inquiry by Source (2019)

	Q1	Q2	Q3	Q4
Organic Web	$ -	$ -	$ -	$ -
Inbound	$ -	$ -	$ -	$ -
PPC Advertising	$ 199	$ 199	$ 199	$ 199
OCS	$ 56	$ 56	$ 56	$ 56
Trade Shows	$ 75	$ 75	$ 75	$ 75
Webinars	$ 63	$ 63	$ 63	$ 63

CONVERSION RATE: Historical Conversion Rates (2019)

Campaign Type	Inquiry to MQL	MQL to TQL	TQL to SAL	SAL to SQL
Organic Web	42%	7%	99%	55%
Inbound	79%	64%	98%	55%
PPC Web	69%	5%	98%	55%
OCS	14%	2%	100%	55%
Trade Shows	30%	5%	96%	55%
Webinars	16%	2%	91%	55%
2020 Goal	34%	11%	97%	65%

Figure 14 Example of a lead flow model using conversions and historical spend to help allocate budget to meet lead goals

53

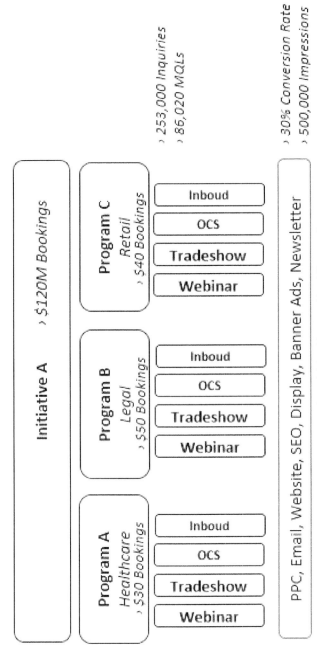

Figure 15 Example of a campaign with bookings and lead flow goals

Initiative A › $120M Bookings

Program A
Healthcare
› $30 Bookings

- Inboud
- OCS
- Tradeshow
- Webinar

Program B
Legal
› $50 Bookings

- Inboud
- OCS
- Tradeshow
- Webinar

Program C
Retail
› $40 Bookings

- Inboud
- OCS
- Tradeshow
- Webinar

PPC, Email, Website, SEO, Display, Banner Ads, Newsletter

› 253,000 Inquiries
› 86,020 MQLs

› 30% Conversion Rate
› 500,000 Impressions

3
Technology

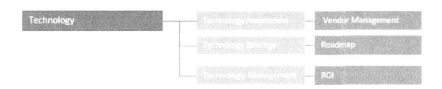

Technology acquisition by a marketing organization was the original driving force for the creation of marketing operations. As I noted earlier, in the early 2000s the advent of SaaS allowed the marketing department to purchase technology without the blessing and review of their IT/IS department. In the early days, that turned out to be a curse as many marketing departments, hoping technology would save them, were burdened with an unworkable tech stack. Marketing quickly learned what IT/IS had learned a long time ago about the total cost of ownership.

In this chapter, we will discuss three crucial topics that all marketing departments must understand before they begin purchasing technology.

Technology Assessment looks at the critical task of choosing a vendor, going through a purchase process, and then properly managing the vendor to maximize ROI. This section will show you how to properly assess your organization's current technology stack and assess new technologies.

Technology Strategy discusses how to set up a roadmap for success. It starts with a thorough assessment of current technologies and then clearly lays out the objectives of the marketing organization as they relate to their technology purchases.

In Technology Management, we look at the various aspects of technology to ensure you are getting the best use of it. Building sound business processes within the technology to increase user adoption and revenue are all discussed in this section.

Before we get started, let's look at marketing technology from a larger perspective so we can understand the difference between demand generation technology and operations technology.

Demand generation technology can be defined as the technology that is used directly in creating demand for an organization's product or services. Services like webinar platforms, Google AdWords, content syndication platforms, email engines (like MAPs), and content experience platforms can all be considered demand generation tools.

Operations technology can be defined as the technology that supports the generation of demand but does not directly contribute to the creation of that demand. Software like lead routing and assignment, BI tools, data appending, response tracking are good examples of operations technology. You will notice in the table below that the MAP falls into both categories. It is because a MAP has a broad technology remit and, when used properly, can solve a myriad of challenges.

The table below gives examples of each category of technology and is by no means meant to be an exhaustive list:

Demand Generation Technologies	Operations Technologies
MAP	MAP
Webinar Platforms	BI Tools
PPC Management	Lead Routing
Content Syndication	Data Appending
Website Personalization	Data Cleansing
Content Experience	Lead Assignment
Data Management Platforms	Response Management
Predictive Technologies	CRM

Typically, the primary users of demand generation technologies are the demand generation team. Those technologies are supported, implemented, and integrated by the operations team but are not generally used by that team. The primary user of operations technologies is the operations team as those technologies are typically foundational to the operations of a marketing organization.

In the following chapters, Ia will be discussing both technologies as they relate to technology strategy and roadmaps, so, it will be helpful to keep these categories in mind.

Technology Assessment

A technology assessment is a critical step to maximize the value of past and current investments, but it is also a guide for future investments in technology solutions. A well-conducted assessment will provide the marketing organization with a clear vision of the current state of technology and a roadmap for a future state.

At some point in the marketing operations journey, there should be a technology assessment conducted. For some organizations, it may be worth conducting once every two to three years. It depends upon the pace of change in the organization, the number of technologies, and the overall complexity of those technologies.

If you are new to the organization and are expected to purchase technology, it would be wise to conduct your assessment before purchasing any new technology. The assessment should include as many stakeholders, primary users, and budget owners as possible and should include people from other departments, as well. Other departmental interviews often give you a different perspective on the overall value that they perceive technology provides. Some other departments to consider are IT/IS, field sales, inside sales, and product.

The assessment touches on an array of questions and it is often most appropriate to capture the answers in a spreadsheet so they can be filtered and analyzed.

	CATEGORY	DESCRIPTION
GENERAL	**User Group**	This refers to the group within marketing that is the primary user of the technology. For instance, the webinar platform is most likely run by your events team while your retargeting software is often run by your digital team.
	Environment	Is it cloud, on-premise, or a third party?
	Function of Technology	This is the primary function of the software.
COST GROUPING	**Annual Cost for Licenses**	This is the cost per user for the licenses if it is a cloud solution. If on-prem, it is typically just a fixed cost.
	Annual Support Cost	The cost of any support contracts. Some solutions require support contracts for anything beyond basic support.
	Annual Professional Services Cost	Advanced features or non-standard integrations usually require professional services. It is very common for the initial purchase to have a package of PS hours bundled into it to make sure the onboarding is successful.
	Training Costs	Some organizations like to purchase training credits to keep their users up to date on the latest features.
	Integration Costs	It is not uncommon for integrations into other software to cost money.
	Total Cost	The total annual cost factoring in all of the above costs.

FUNCTIONAL GROUPING	**User Adoption**	Measures how well the tool is used among its primary user group.
	Importance	Measures how important the tool is to the functions of the organization. For instance, the marketing automation platform is often a must-have for modern marketing departments.
	Feature/ Function Alignment	How well do the features align with the strategy of the marketing organization?
	Extensibility	Is the technology extensible and scalable?
	Data	How secure is the data? Is it PI? Are there extra charges for data storage? If so, capture those in costs.
	Integrated	Does it integrate into the necessary software to provide automated processes between systems?

Figure 1 The three functional areas of software assessment and their discrete categories.

You can create three groups. The first group focuses on general questions about the software. The second calculates all of the associated costs of the software. The final group focuses on the functions and features of the software. For the third group, you can come up with a simple rating system that allows you to rank each category from the best to the worst. I like to use a scale of 1–5. For example, if you give a 5 to importance, then the software is of critical importance to the marketing organization. If you give a 1 to integrated then the software is probably siloed.

With both scoring and cost information prepared, it is a relatively easy task to begin capturing the output in an excel spreadsheet.

Figure 2 shows what the cost category might look like.

Cost				
Training Cost	Integration Cost	License Cost	Support Cost	Total Annual Cost
$ 1,000.00	$ 20,000.00	$ 79,000.00	$ 20,000.00	$ 120,000.00
$ 500.00	$ 1,000.00	$ 100,000.00	$ 10,000.00	$ 111,500.00
$ 2,000.00	$ 1,000.00	$ 10,000.00	$ 15,000.00	$ 28,000.00
$ 500.00	$ -	$ 50,000.00	$ 5,000.00	$ 55,500.00
$ 1,000.00	$ 1,000.00	$ 40,000.00	$ 1,000.00	$ 43,000.00
$ 2,000.00	$ -	$ 70,000.00	$ -	$ 72,000.00
$ 1,500.00	$ -	$ 20,100.00	$ 4,000.00	$ 25,600.00
$ 1,000.00	$ -	$ 36,000.00		$ 37,000.00

Figure 2 An example of the cost category

The functional group assesses the importance of the technology by ranking it on five criteria. How important is the software to the strategy of the marketing organization? Does it have all of the features needed? Is it integrated into other technologies? They are all important questions when considering the overall adoption of the technology. You can rank each criterion on a scale of 1 to 5 as well, with 1 being not used at all and 5 being heavily used.

The functional group should be averaged to arrive at an average functional score. You can see an example of the functional group in Figure 3 on the following page.

Function					
Importance	Features	Extensibility	Data	Integrated	Avg.
2	3	1	4	3	2.60
3	2	1	5	5	3.20
1	2	3	5	3	2.80
3	4	5	2	5	3.80
5	5	5	5	5	5.00
4	4	4	4	5	4.20
3	3	3	3	1	2.60

Figure 3 An example of the functional category

It is often helpful to score both the total cost and functional average on a chart with the high cost and high function falling into the upper right quadrant and low usage and function falling into the lower left. The technologies that fall on the left side of the graph should be looked at for replacement or end of life.

With the assessment complete, you can properly assess new technologies and how they will enhance your current stack or replace older less-used technologies.

Technology Selection

You must select the correct technology based upon an honest evaluation of the needs of the organization. Choosing an immature technology that cannot meet your most complex requirements is just as bad as choosing a mature one that is too complicated for the resources you have dedicated to it.

The four steps to selecting a technology are:

1. Requirements gathering
2. Technology Assessment

3. Negotiation
4. Renewal

Requirement Gathering

The Requirements Gathering stage should focus on two objectives: solution requirements and research. The final output of the requirements gathering stage should be a requirements document that details the features, functions, and price range the intended solution should meet. You will also narrow your potential vendors down to a list of three or four based on peer reviews, research, and analyst reports.

Technology Assessment

In this stage, you will set up demos with each vendor that was identified in the previous step. During the demonstration focus on the functions and features within the requirements document. Make sure you understand each vendor's solution enough to rank them in a vendor comparison table as shown in Figure 4. In the example, the vendors are being compared on two features, support, and training.

Vendor	Cost	Feature 1		F2		Support		Training		Total Score
1	$ 15,000	5		5		5		4		4.8
2	$ 10,000	2		4		4		5		3.8
3	$ 12,000	3	25%	2	25%	3	25%	0	25%	2.0
4	$ 13,500	1		0		4		4		2.3
5	$ 5,000	1		0		4		2		1.8

Figure 4 Example of technology assessment

63

Once weights are applied, it can be helpful to map out the scores and price on a matrix to see where the vendors rank (as we did in the technology assessment section with current vendors). As in the previous section, we can split the matrix into four quadrants. The upper right quadrant are vendors that are good fits but expensive while the lower right are vendors that should be engaged. Vendors on the left lack the functionality to be considered. You can plot the table above by total score and cost as shown in Figure 5.

Use the matrix to narrow down your vendors to one or two. It might make sense to set up another demo for greater clarity on features if you are still undecided.

If you have decided upon a vendor you can move to the next stage

Figure 5 Matrix of technology scores to assess the viability of proposed solutions

Negotiation

After deciding upon a final vendor, the next step is to negotiate contract pricing, terms, and conditions and then to execute the contract. In my many years of negotiating contracts, I can share some helpful tips:

- **Timing Matters** The end of the quarter or end of the year for vendors are important times. They are looking to close as much business as possible during those final weeks to make sure they achieve their booking goal. The vendor will be more agreeable to discounts during those periods. Just make sure you are indeed ready to sign as the discount will come with an expiration date from the vendor.

- **Competitors Matter** If a vendor finds out you are also considering a competitor, they might be more apt to give discounts. This is especially true if the space in which they compete is still in a growth phase and each vendor is looking for market share. It is also the case if you are currently using a competitor and your purchase will be replacing them.

- **Terms Matter** The length of the contract can also be a good leverage point for vendors. Nowadays, a lot of vendors are pressing for a three-year contract, but some vendors remain flexible. Their flexibility often depends on their internal emphasis on Annual Contract Value (ACV) or Total Contract

Value (TCV). If the vendor is focused on ACV, then you can often front-load the first year and receive discounts on the subsequent years. If TCV is more important, you can usually get bigger discounts for the longer terms.

- **References Matter** Sometimes, if you are a large company or have an enviable logo, the company will ask you to be a reference for them in the future. You can often use that as leverage to negotiate better terms.

Renewal

The final phase is understanding when the renewal is up and the cancellation terms of the vendor. Most, if not all, vendors require at least a thirty-day notice for cancellation and some of the vendors I have worked with require ninety days. It is helpful to have a central place for all technology contracts with their cancellation policy noted and the renewal date. If you have done an appropriate inventory, as noted in the first part of this section, you should already have the information handy.

On my staff, I usually have each employee own certain technologies that align with their role. They become the expert on the technology but also are responsible for the renewal and management of the vendor with my guidance. It allows them to begin to understand the complexities of vendor management, contract negotiations, and technology support at an early point in their careers.

Technology Strategy

Demand Generation Technology

One of the foundational pieces of a good marketing strategy is the technology that is relied upon to execute. I have been in many organizations, especially in the early days of SaaS, that devoured technology at a rapid pace because they were allured by the features and promise of easy success only to see the technology sit underutilized. To avoid unused technology, it is important to understand the four components that influence the purchase of demand generation technology:

1. Your business/industry maturity
2. Your target market and persona
3. Your offering type
4. Your marketing contribution

1. Business Maturity

It is critical to understand your organizational maturity and the maturity of your industry. Both factors should influence any technology you buy because choosing a technology that is not aligned to the business can cause budget issues or hinder growth. Figure 6 is a simple illustration of the maturity of a business over time

Every company goes through five stages of maturity and the same could be said for industries, as well. In the initial launch phase, there is low growth, negative cash flow, and low profit as a company establishes a market presence and refines its offering. The growth stage is accompanied by high spending to fund the growth and that results in low cash and profit. Somewhere toward the tail end of the growth stage, if the company is fortunate, they will see positive cash flow and profits.

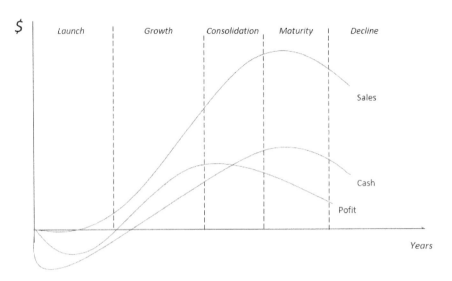

Figure 6 Lifecycle of a company with cash, profit, and sales plotted

Many companies never make it to that stage. However, once that happens, most industries and companies see consolidation in both their offerings and in their industry as other organizations and competitors move into the space and buy up companies to eliminate offerings. Eventually—like all good things—as technology changes, markets change and the consumer changes and there is an inevitable decline. You can use the knowledge of those stages to help guide your technology budgets. The table on the following page summarizes the stages and the type of technology strategy which should be utilized.

	Marketing Strategy	Spend	Technology
Launch	Refining messaging & target persona	Tight budgets, high scrutiny	A/B testing, content syndication, website
Growth	Brand exposure, drive pipeline	High spend	MAP, CRM, PRM funnel measurement, data appending & lead routing
Consolidation	Moving up segments, efficient spending, refined tactics	Consolidate spend on high ROI techs,	Consolidate on CRM or MAP applications,
Maturity	Focus on profitability, efficient spending, a higher focus on existing customers	Spend remains flat,	BI tools, sales enablement tools, customer advocacy
Decline	Retaining existing customers, cost-cutting	Reduced spend, tight budgets	End of life old technologies, technology consolidation,

Figure 8 Matrix of marketing and technology strategy at different points in a company lifecycle

2. Target Market

Each target market has its characteristics. Marketing should thoroughly understand their target market before making any technology purchases. An obvious example is GDPR in Europe. Any technology that collects contact information in a non-compliant way would be at best a waste of time and at worst could result in a large fine for the organization. Understanding how your target audience interacts with buyers is essential as well.

In one of my first companies, we targeted salespeople who are notoriously outgoing and will answer their phones. We invested in a large outbound calling program that targeted those individuals with success because we understood their preferences. Conversely, at a different company I worked for, we targeted IS and IT buyers who rarely answer their phones, are concerned with privacy and security, and are not as outgoing as a group. That group relied on their peers and tight social groups to get recommendations for technology purchases. As a result, we targeted peer review sites like G2 Crowd and IT Central Station. In addition, we invested heavily in analyst relations to gain third-party recognition in the marketplace.

3. Product Type

The type of product or service you sell also has a large impact on your technology strategy. The three product types that require specific go-to-market strategies are the new entrant, disruptive solution, and mature player. Figure 9 on the following page defines each type and illustrates their distinctive needs.

a. New Entrant

A new entrant means your offering is brand new into a market and has no market awareness that can be leveraged to help buyers. Most buyers will not even understand the problem that is being solved and will most certainly not have budget allocated. Combined, these two factors make it certain that the sales cycle will be longer, and that more education is required.

The impact on your technology strategy is apparent. You will need technology that can disseminate educational content widely, target a wide array of personas at a high volume, and be able to nurture the buyers over a longer time. Below is a list of technologies that are suited for that type of offering.

TYPE	TECHNOLOGY	PURPOSE
NEW ENTRANT	*MAP*	*Long Term Nurture*
	Webinars	*Education*
	PPC	*High volume, low-cost targeting*
	Content Syndication	*Targeted Education*

Figure 9 Technology needs of new entrant product type

b. Disruptive Solution

A disruptive solution is typically a new way of solving an old problem. It can be at a significant cost reduction that disrupts the pricing and margin structure of competing organizations, or it can be a completely new way of addressing an established problem. Either way, a disruptive solution, unlike a new entrant, has an established market and awareness of the problem being solved. As a result, the technologies used for a disruptive solution differ slightly because the target market is well defined, and budgets have been established.

TYPE	TECHNOLOGY	PURPOSE
DISRUPTIVE SOLUTION	*MAP*	*Short Term nurture*
	Webinars	*Mid funnel targeting*
	PPC	*Target market*
	Content Syndication	*Vendor Rankings, Mid funnel*
	Predictive Analytics	*Account Targeting*

Figure 10 Technology needs of a disruptive solution product type

c. **Mature Player**

I like to call this area the red ocean. Market share is hard to win, prices are already low, and many competitors are targeting each other. Growth comes from seeking out margins and displacing competitors which is hard to do since no one solution is that much better than another.

TYPE	TECHNOLOGY	PURPOSE
MATURE PLAYER	*MAP*	*High Volume discount targeting*
	Webinars	*Bottom funnel*
	DMP	*High volume bottom-funnel*
	Content Syndication	*Vendor Rankings, bottom-funnel*
	Intent Signals	*Competitor Targeting*
	Trade shows	*Brand awareness*

Figure 11 Technology needs of a mature player product type

4. Marketing Contribution

The final consideration for technology strategy is the expected contribution from Marketing. How much a marketing organization is expected to contribute to an organization's revenue will have a major impact on demand technology decisions. The more the marketing organization is expected to source and influence, the more technologies the marketing organization will need to procure.

Operations Technology

Operations technology has different considerations that affect its roadmap. When purchasing operations technology, you must have the additional considerations of staffing and resources, sales structure, and organizational complexity.

1. Staffing and Resources

How experienced are the employees in deploying and supporting technology? Are they experienced enough to solve business problems with technology? What is the long-term plan to hire marketing operations people? Does the marketing operations staff report to a manager or are they rolled into the demand generation team?

2. Sales Structure

Another important consideration is the size and makeup of the sales organization. A large field sales force is different to support than an inside sales group. Does the sales organization employ BDRs that qualify leads before handing them to a salesperson?

3. Organizational Complexity

For lack of a better term, complexity can mean size, product set, market conditions, go-to-market motions, and a host of other factors. For example, in my first job, we were a relatively simple organization with one product, inside sales, and a single source of truth in our CRM. A small technology stack with a few supporting tools was all we needed. Conversely, when I worked at a Fortune 500 company, we had multiple business units, several databases inherited from acquisitions that were considered the truth for those units, and complex channel requirements.

Technology Management

The primary responsibility of the MOPs team is to ensure that the marketing organization is getting the most out of its technology. In other words, that the ROI is positive. The marketing department, as well as the entire organization, must see the impact and return of the various tools being used. As the largest consumer of technology, the MOPs team needs to be able to show the impact their purchases have on the organization.

There are three main factors to consider when trying to fully leverage a technology:

1. Business process integration
2. User adoption
3. Revenue impact

1. Business Process Integration

Business process integration is the ability to leverage a technology to support a business process rather than just tactical outputs. The MAP technology is a perfect example of a tool that is commonly used for tactical outputs like email, landing pages, and forms when it can support complex business requirements. Let's take a closer look at some of the ways a MAP platform can be used to build business processes.

Lead Scoring

While not a complex use case, lead scoring is one of the easiest ways to build value within your MAP platform. Lead scoring is easily built by assigning scores to digital touches and then adding up those touches into a total score. After a certain score has been achieved, the lead is then routed to a team for follow-up and further qualification.

Most companies use some combination of activity scoring combined with firmographic scoring to arrive at a priority level for the lead. In its most basic form, the activity level is rated on a 1 to 4 scale and the firmographic score is rated from A to D. Thus, your A1s would be your best leads, meeting both a high activity level and a high firmographic score.

I won't spend too much time on lead scoring as there is a ton of literature out there already on how to score leads via your MAP platform. However, I would like to point out that scoring leads with firmographics can lead to missed leads as data is often not complete enough to arrive at a confident firmographic score.

For example, a director-level lead at a large company may fill out the form and give wrong information, resulting in a lower firmographic score. If you are relying on the firmographic score to route leads, you might miss that lead. In my opinion, to avoid that situation, it is best to use the digital activity as your main filter and have someone follow up to confirm the firmographic fit.

Lead Nurturing

While lead nurturing is based on tactical activities, it should be a strategic consideration as it is the main way to turn top-of-the-funnel inquiries into purchases, creating long-term ROI on your demand generation investments. Strategic nurturing is more than just sending out some emails every week to your database to keep in touch until they are ready to buy.

A good nurturing program should be a multi-tiered approach to segment a prospect's needs and deliver the correct message and content. Figure 12 illustrates an example of a multi-tiered nurture approach that drives a prospect through several tiers to reach a targeted message.

A well-constructed nurture track will be able to measure the amount of revenue it influences. I think the best way to attribute revenue back to nurture tracks is to add prospects to the nurture campaign only if they view the content. Doing it that way allows you to be sure the prospect engaged in content and was not merely flowing through the track.

Funnel Tracking

Funnel tracking refers to the process of tracking prospects as they progress through a funnel toward their final disposition. At each stage, a prospect can be disqualified or pass through to the next stage based on certain predefined criteria.

One of the most common methodologies for funnel tracking was developed by Sirius Decisions, a B2B advisory firm. Most organizations adopt some version of their waterfall tracking. I like their Rearchitected Waterfall that they created several years ago which includes a Telequalified Lead (TQL) stage. The addition of TQL makes allowances for an SDR team qualifying leads and passing them to a sales team.

An in-depth discussion on how to build out funnel tracking is beyond the scope of this book, but I will give you some of the things I have learned over the years.

1. As a prospect passes through each stage, make sure you are date stamping the entry. I have seen some systems date stamping both the entry and exit but, at the very least, you will need to make sure you are date stamping the entry.

2. If a lead is passing from one buying stage to another, there should be acceptance criteria established before the lead is moved into the next stage. This is the reason

78

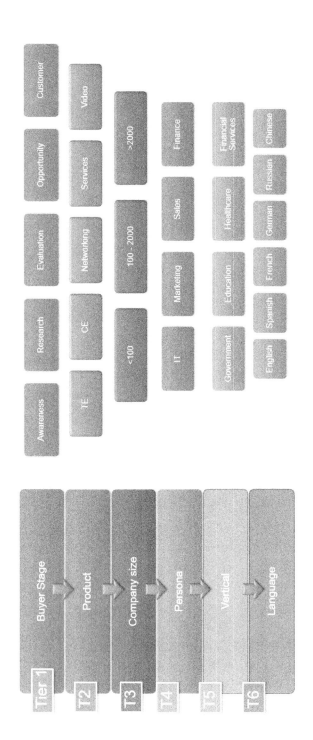

Figure 12 An example of a lead nurturing program

for tele-accepted leads (TAL) and sales-accepted leads (SAL). It is a critical step because it ensures the system is within governance.

As a basic example, if your sales team is only supposed to accept red leads for qualification, they need to make sure the lead is red before trying to qualify it. If they accept blue leads, as well, or maybe one rep accepts blue and red, when you try to assess the performance of your demand generation engine, you will not be able to effectively measure the performance because the system was out of governance.

Make sure your reps are only accepting and working the type of leads that you have defined as a group.

3. Create discrete stages that have only one entry criterion. If you have a stage with multiple entry criteria, then identifying performance and patterns from reporting will be virtually impossible. When looking at anomalies in conversions between stages, you must be able to accurately deduce what is wrong by comparing conversations.

Campaign Attribution

Campaign attribution is one of the most important things to build correctly as it is the primary way that a marketing organization will prove value. Understanding what campaigns are creating the most revenue for your sales team is not only important for optimizing spending but also in securing more budget.

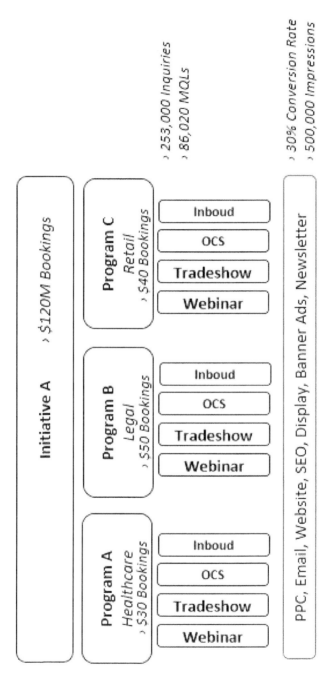

Figure 13 Campaign hierarchy example

Campaign attribution requires carefully architected activities within your MAP system so you can tie engagement back to the correct activity and then link that engagement through the waterfall to the prospect's final disposition. If we look back to Chapter 1 when we discussed campaign funding, you will remember the diagram in Figure 13.

The architecture can be leveraged again to create proper attribution at all levels of your marketing spend. When set up correctly in your MAP and CRM, tactics at the bottom can be linked to activities like webinars, tradeshows, OCS, and inbound. Those activities are then rolled into their corresponding programs and up to the Initiative. Spend can also be aggregated at each level, as well, so you can calculate efficiency metrics like cost per and ROI.

The details of how this is built are beyond the scope of this book but below are some of the most common ways it can be achieved:

1. Use UTM codes and/or referrer IDs. That allows you to tag each tactic and/or activity with a specific code to identify in your MAP and/or CRM.

2. Use the campaign hierarchy that is native to your CRM. Set up campaign types that reflect the campaign structure you built. For example, having campaign record types of initiative, program, and activity would make sense for the diagram above.

3. Capture spend on the campaign records of each of the types and do so as accurately as possible. Often, you can have the demand generation team put in an amount or you can have an operations person reconcile

the spend at the end of the quarter with your accounting system.

4. Setting up your accounting GLs so they align to your activities is often an easy way to link spending correctly back to your activities and then you can use a code to identify the tactic within that activity.

User Adoption

Traditionally, organizations focused on user adoption with an activity-based definition that measures whether and how often end-users log in to the tools or enter data. While the number of logins is a tangible indicator of use, it is not evidence of usefulness or meaningful adoption. A better way to measure user adoption recognizes the value that can be gained from technology investments beyond the number of users and logins.

User adoption can be assessed on a spectrum of five stages:

1. **Unknown:** At that stage, end users are generally unaware of the tool or technology. It may be older technology.

2. **Pilot:** A pilot program is a test and proof of concept or a prototype of a system, technology, or process before general availability.

3. **Implemented**: Users are aware of the technology but have not yet integrated it into workflows or processes. Logins are low and adoption is low.

4. **Mature:** The technology is used daily and is recognized as an important function in a marketing organization's tactical activities. The technology is

more than likely integrated into at least one other software and people outside of the marketing organization are aware of its use.

5. **Strategic**: Strategic technologies are fully integrated into an organization's business processes and are often leveraged by other departments to fulfill some of their strategic goals. The technology is referred to at the highest level of the organization and is understood to be an integral part of a company's success.

You can measure adoption in three ways:

1. **Usage**: Usage metrics are easily obtained by the system administrator. Some of the more common ones are the number of licenses; number of logins per day, week, and month; number of activities completed; and duration of login time. Each technology might have a different measure of usage, so, it is important to understand the technology before creating a set of usage metrics.

2. **Data quality:** Some simple data quality metrics include completed key data fields, the accuracy of data, duplicate records, and automated data processing.

3. **Integrations:** How many integrations are supported with the technology? How many strategic initiatives does it support? For example, marketing automation software that supports nurturing, lead scoring, funnel stage tracking, and campaign attribution is more valuable than software that simply sends emails and tracks web activity.

Revenue Impact

Measuring the revenue impact of technology is the best way to prove ROI. The executive staff will be much more willing to pay a higher price on renewal if the technology is widely known to impact revenue. Some of the easiest ways to do that are to make sure that you have strategic business processes integrated into the technology as we covered in the previous section.

By optimizing the collection of revenue, marketing technology can reduce the overall cost it takes to recognize revenue. There are several ways marketing technology can achieve that with the four processes outlined in the previous section.

Lead Nurturing

Lead nurturing can increase velocity and deal size. You can easily measure that by comparing closed won deals that have nurture touches to those that do not.

Lead Scoring

Effective lead scoring can increase down funnel conversions, making it so your SDR staff can be smaller and more efficient. If your SDRs are qualifying more than 10 percent of the prospects they are talking with, then you have a good scoring program that saves the organization money on SDR staffing.

Funnel Tracking

The ability to track a customer from the top of the funnel to their final disposition is a very visible way to show technology ROI. You cannot optimize your revenue collection without knowing when and why prospects are dropping out of the funnel. Understanding conversion rates at each stage and being able to adjust SLAs, entry, and exit criteria is very valuable to an organization.

Campaign Attribution

Optimizing campaign spending is nearly impossible without a way to track revenue back to campaign activities. Technologies that let the demand generation group understand what activities to increase spending in, and what activities need to be stopped, are invaluable. You can easily measure ROI on those by tracking CPL and various other costs per metric.

4
Support and Administration

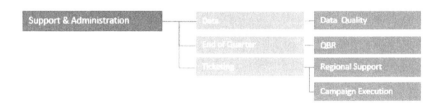

Not all marketing operations consist of building exciting processes that solve complex business problems or the implementation of trendy technologies. The bulk of marketing operations is spent servicing and supporting the marketing organization so that they can generate revenue for the company.

The MO group should have a ticketing system or some other work tracking process. The support a marketing operations group provides for a marketing organization can generally fall into three categories:

1. Data
2. End of quarter
3. Ticketing

Data

Data quality is a struggle for all organizations. Forrester estimates that the amount of prospect and customer data in the average organization doubles every twelve to eighteen months and, without a maintenance process, clean data quickly deteriorates. Their research shows that between 10 percent and 25 percent of their records include critical data errors like bad email, phone, and title.[14]

It's easy to get lost in the myriad of statistics surrounding the importance of data quality. But, as insightful as statistics may be, I find the 1–10–100 rule to be the easiest to grasp and remember. It depicts the high costs associated with the endless cycle of using bad data to run your business.

The basis of the rule is very simple. It takes $1 to verify a record as it is entered, $10 to cleanse it, and $100 if nothing is done. The ramifications of the mistakes are felt for as long as the data goes unaddressed. It shows what many fail to realize about data quality which is that poor data quality isn't a one-off problem. Your organization is losing money and it can impact strategic decisions. If you doubt the $100 cost, here is a quick list of all the things bad data impacts:

1. Emailing to wrong address and impact on sender score
2. Losing disgruntled customers

---

[14] Forrester "The Impact of Bad Data on Demand Unit Management"2019

3. Sales conflict over same leads
4. Inability to track the lead source and marketing attribution
5. Incorrect segmentation and personalization
6. Unnecessary MAP and CRM costs for duplicate records
7. Misguided strategic decisions based on poor demand unit analysis

It is by no means an exhaustive list and I am sure you can think of many more. Given the list above, $100 seems a conservative estimate.

Figure 1 Cost of bad data

The above graph illustrates the cost of bad data assuming data grows yearly by 40 percent and 25 percent of it is bad. You can see how the cost of keeping bad data grows in the system each year.

Ensuring good data quality, as shown above, will have a measurable impact on your marketing organization's performance. There are several tools available to help with data quality. I have included a table below to help you understand what service each one performs and the impact of that service.

Name	Service	Impact
Data Appending	Data appending is integrated directly into your MAP or CRM and corrects and fills in data	Better segmentation
Email Verification	Script on form capture	Improved Sender Score and lower data storage costs
Lead Matching/De-Duping	Data service software that can de-dupe, match, attach leads to accounts, etc.	Better segmentation, less sales conflict

Figure 2 Data services and their impact

Ending the Quarter

The end of the quarter is a busy time for MO as they wrap up a quarter and transition to a new one. Several tasks need to be undertaken to make the transition. I have separated them into two categories. The first are tasks that are required to end the quarter and the second are tasks that are required to start the new quarter.

89

Ending the Quarter

1. Campaign costs
2. QBR decks
3. Data loading and correction

Starting the Quarter

1. Creating new quarterly campaigns and/or programs
2. Aligning on quarterly priorities
3. Updating the UTMs if necessary

Campaign Costs

To calculate ROI on your marketing activities, you must have a reliable way for campaign costs to be entered into the system. The most common way is for people to use the salesforce campaign object which has a designated place for those costs. If you remember the campaign hierarchy from previous chapters, a salesforce campaign is equal to an activity. You should also have your campaigns set up in such a way that you can roll it up to a program and initiative. Having the campaign costs on the record gives you an easy way to calculate all of your costs per information for your ROI. Here are some examples:

1. Cost per waterfall Unit
2. Cost per name
3. Cost per activity, tactic, program, and initiative
4. Return on pipeline (Pipeline ROI)
5. Return on bookings (Bookings ROI)
6. Return on program, activity, and tactic

QBR Decks

Most marketing departments and most departments, for that matter, conduct quarterly business reviews (QBR). Typically, they happen sometime during the second or third week of the next quarter which gives MO time to prepare the deck and the finance department time to close the books.

QBRs are a great way to review previous quarters' performance against KPIs, monitor campaign performance, adjust strategy, and make sure the whole department is knowledgeable about the business of marketing. A typical QBR will cover the following items and, if you have regions, all the metrics will be split by regions:

1. Bookings and pipeline against budget
2. Trending QoQ bookings and pipeline
3. Waterfall conversion rates against target and industry benchmarks
4. Campaign performance down to activities and tactics

Data Loading and Correction

It is important to make sure that all the data is correct and complete before creating a QBR deck. Physical events are often the largest source of incomplete data as the list often takes a long time to be received and loaded. Be careful to make sure all events are loaded into the appropriate campaigns with the correct costs before doing any campaign analysis. Additionally, you may have to wait for your finance department to finalize its books, so spending is properly allocated and bookings numbers are finalized. Finalizing numbers may take about a week after the quarter is complete and, therefore, it is important to be in close coordination with your finance department.

Starting the Quarter

Creating new quarterly campaigns and/or programs

The start of the quarter should always involve creating new campaigns and programs as needed. A meeting with the demand generation teams is appropriate to understand any new programs or campaigns which will be started in the upcoming quarter.

Aligning quarterly priorities

If you are doing sprint planning, the beginning of the quarter is the appropriate time to discuss any large projects that will need to be completed during the quarter. New technologies to install, new processes to architect, and/or large trade shows or campaign launches are all important to discuss to make sure operations are aligned on the priorities of their internal customers.

Updating dashboards

KPIs for the upcoming quarter should be discussed and recorded. Quarterly dashboards in your CRM or BI tool should be updated and new dashboards to capture any new KPIs should be created. The operations team should focus on completing those tasks within the first week of the quarter.

Ticketing

Depending on how large your MO group is, you may or may not require a ticketing system. Smaller organizations often let the field teams create email campaigns and segmentation within the MAP. However, as an organization grows, the need for a more centralized process will arise as the organization desires more metrics.

The ticketing platform will allow the organization to request campaigns, email programs, data fixes, dashboards, reports, landing pages, list loads, and event and webinar support. A good ticketing platform will allow MO to understand what requests take the longest and how many requests they receive in a given period which will help establish SLAs.

5
Process Design and Management

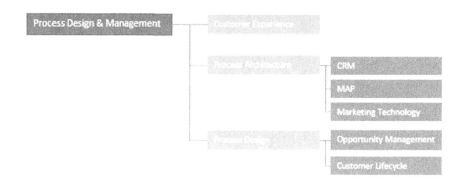

Process design and the management of processes is one of the most important functions of MO. An efficient and thoughtful process can move a marketing organization forward in maturity while a poorly designed and inefficient process can, at best, hinder an organization and, at worst, call into question all the data and metrics being created.

Everyone wants to create good processes and deliver value to an organization but what makes a good process? Would you be able to recognize a good process if you saw one? I think it is relatively easy to identify a bad process but only after it has been built and is creating problems. How do you stop bad processes from being built and ensure that good processes are designed?

In my twenty years of experience conducting process design, I have established two core tenants of all good process design. A good process must:

1. Deliver something of value to the organization
2. Align with corporate values and strategy

Let's look at each one of those tenants to see how it creates good processes.

Deliver something of value to someone outside of the process.

A good process must solve a business problem that an organization is experiencing. Stay away from designing processes looking for problems. All good process design begins with an excellent understanding of the desired outcome. The desired outcome should be put into a process value statement that does not include any mention of technology. A good process value statement will include several things:

1. What is trying to be solved?
2. Why is it being solved?
3. What will be the desired outputs from the process?

It is often necessary to create a list from the various stakeholders of those desired outputs to capture them correctly. They should be listed in the design statement in the order of priority or must-haves and nice to have.

Let's look at an example of a good process design statement for a demand waterfall design on the following page. It will contain answers to all three of the questions above.

The marketing organization needs a way to track prospects through the buying process from inquiry until hand-off to the sales organization. The process will allow the marketing organization to evaluate its impact on revenue by understanding campaign effectiveness, SDR performance, funnel efficiency, and spend optimization.

Desired Outputs:

Must-Haves:

- Conversion tracking through each stage
- Velocity calculations for each stage
- Campaign attribution
- Expense tracking on campaigns
- ROI calculations by campaign, program, activity, and tactic
- SDR call activity tracking

Nice to Have:

- Different attribution models
- Regional differences in funnel tracking

By enabling the marketing department to better understand its spend on-demand generation activities, the process delivers value by helping the organization become more profitable by increasing ROI on marketing activities.

Align with corporate strategy

A process that is not aligned with a corporate strategy will fail to sustain itself. During my early career when I ran the operations for a smaller B2B organization, I encountered this issue when trying to build a quick onboarding process for our partners. The idea was sound: to give potential partners an easy and quick way to sign up to resell our products without a lot of human interaction. More often than not, those partners were small and the fewer resources we spent on getting them signed up and selling, the more profitable the relationship.

I worked diligently over a couple of months to design a form, a landing page, and a routing tree that allowed partners to fill out a form and receive information about being a partner. If they decided to sign up for our partner program, they could process their application with another online form that walked them through the necessary forms to begin selling our products. We even provided them with training and affiliate links they could use to promote our products to their network.

It was early in my career and I was excited to build processes that required integrating data flow between several systems, so, I never stopped and asked if this was a corporate strategy. It was not until the process was finished and launched that I learned that our partner strategy was to align with two or three large resellers and put all our effort into those rather than signing as many small partners as we could. Unbeknownst to me, we had already signed up one of the largest partners in the space and they wound up being responsible for nearly 45 percent of the revenue we generated as a company.

Needless to say, the beautiful and carefully architected process I had built was never used and I had wasted nearly an entire quarter. It was a good lesson to learn early in my career that even the most thoughtfully designed process will not be used if it does not align with corporate objectives.

Building and Designing Process

Once you have confirmed the process intended to be designed has met the two core tenants as outlined above, you can move forward with the design and build. Below are the nine steps that all good process designs must follow:

1. Requirements and business strategy
2. Process governance
3. Process architecture and structure
4. Performance management
5. Documentation
6. Implementation and change management
7. IT alignment
8. Monitoring
9. Continuous improvement

Requirements and Business Strategy

Gathering requirements and aligning with business strategy are important first steps. Gathering requirements includes meeting with all stakeholders, fully understanding the problem to be solved, and key dependencies.

Different from aligning with corporate strategy, it is understanding the foundational business strategy that the process is supporting. The business strategy is focused on the need of the specific business group you are supporting. Using a lead management process as an example, you can understand how tracking leads through the funnel and reporting on ROI is a critical business strategy for marketing.

Process Governance

Any well-built process will have the ability to be properly governed to make sure it is aligned with expected inputs, outputs, and SLAs. Early in my career, I built a process that failed to govern the expected inputs and therefore could not properly measure expected outputs.

The first lead management process I built was designed around scored leads being sent to sales reps so they could qualify the prospects over the phone. The sales reps were then instructed to either convert the lead to an opportunity within our CRM or disqualify the lead with a reason. Our MAP was responsible for scoring the leads up to a 1 or 2 to meet the criteria to be sent to a salesperson.

Simple in design—but I forgot to build in governance between the lead score stage and the point at which the salesperson would engage the lead. Two months into the process, I discovered something had happened with the MAP routing and leads of scores 3 and 4 were also being sent to the salespeople. The leads were outside of the expected input criteria. As a result, I had salespeople calling leads that did not meet the agreed-upon scoring threshold and the salespeople were, therefore, performing poorly. When I went to analyze the performance of the funnel, I realized I had unqualified leads being engaged with and it was throwing off our conversion rates because the lead should not have been processed. It made it hard to compare salesperson performance because some reps received more of these bad leads than others.

Needless to say, the process was out of governance with expected inputs and, therefore, I could not measure outputs in a meaningful way. I immediately corrected the problem by having the salespeople confirm the correct score before engaging with the record by accepting the lead with a lead status change. I learned one of the most basic tenants of any process: When inputs cross into another function, they must always be checked to make sure they meet the established acceptance criteria. I liken it to an assembly line that works on assembling parts before the next part is placed. There must be a check to make sure the previous part was placed correctly or your process is out of governance.

Process Architecture and Structure

Perhaps the part we all enjoy the most is the designing and building of the process. I find the best place to do that is within workflow software that can lay out each step and the decision rules that accompany them. The main guidance I can provide here is to make sure you are not grouping several distinct tasks into one step. You are more prone to miss critical decision points. It is often helpful to show a draft of the workflow to someone who does not understand the process and has an eye for detail. Here are some other guiding principles I use when designing processes in systems:

1. Let the system of record do the processing of the data. For example, if you use a CRM and leads are being tracked in the CRM, let your CRM do the status changes and date stamping. It can be done by your MAP but that would mean unnecessarily moving data back and forth between the systems to sync the data.

2. Eliminate as much data syncing where possible. Do not move data back and forth from your MAP to your CRM unless necessary to achieve the desired task.

3. When building processes with multiple steps, build each step and then test the step. Link the completed steps together at the end, knowing each step has been tested independently. Troubleshooting is much easier as a result because you have minimized the number of variables.

4. Be agile in your process build. Build it simple and get it into production as fast as possible to accept feedback into the system. Course correct and add on as more requirements are seen.

Performance Management

No process should be built without the result in mind. Typically, that result is the measurement of some kind of performance. In the example of a lead management system, it is the performance of the marketing leads being measured. Reporting and KPIs should be established upfront and their measurement should be in mind at each step of the architecture. Remember, KPIs are a core part of a good process value statement.

Documentation

You will find that some people on your team have a knack for good documentation. The process of documentation achieves two main purposes. It gives the organization a living document that will be updated each time a change or update is made to the process which is important because most processes outlive their designer. Secondly, good documentation will force someone to go through the process step by step and try to explain it to another person who is most likely not familiar with it. You can sometimes uncover flaws through the process of documentation.

Implementation and Change Management

No process is done after it is released into production. Implementation takes training and education. Hopefully, with the proper KPIs in place and the proper governance, that part is mostly about discipline and repetition. If you have done your homework up-front, your stakeholders should be expecting the changes.

Proper change management takes an excess of communication before and after a release. Repetition is key along with proper monitoring of your governance reports.

IT Alignment

Sometimes processes that marketing operations will design and implement cross over into IT's world. It is important to assess the impact on IT before beginning a project and to get their alignment should you need any support.

Continuous Improvement

Approach process building with a curiosity mindset. When stakeholders approach you with suggestions and/or feedback, take the opportunity to learn and improve instead of defending. Process building is often a complex symphony between several systems and unexpected inputs. Things will break and data will be out of sync. If you keep a curiosity mindset and the understanding that our systems are imperfect, you will have the correct attitude.

6
Business Intelligence and Data

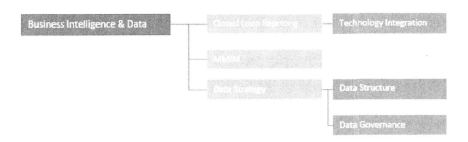

Business Intelligence

Business intelligence (BI) is a close second, right behind process architecture, as my favorite marketing operations discipline. In this chapter, BI is not a technology but rather the use of data to make intelligent and future-looking decisions. Good business intelligence moves beyond activity measurement and helps drive outcomes for a marketing department. Too often, marketing departments struggle with the perception of being a cost center instead of a revenue driver. Outcome-focused analytics can help shift that perception and position marketing as a knowledgeable business partner within an organization.

Business Intelligence is comprised of technologies and strategies used to analyze existing business data to provide future guidance on how best to allocate marketing investments. Good business intelligence is actionable in that it provides data that is not only accurate but aligns with an organization's strategies. Business intelligence does not tell organizations what to do or what will happen if they take a certain course but neither is BI solely about generating reports. Rather, BI offers a way for people to examine data to understand trends and derive insights by streamlining the effort needed to search for, merge, and query the data necessary to make sound business decisions.

The three core components of good BI are closed-loop reporting, the Marketing Measurement Framework (MMF) for continuous improvement, and data. All three together allow you to achieve the ultimate purpose of BI which is to forecast your business so you can make the proper course corrections in the present and make the proper future investments with your marketing dollars.

Closed-Loop Reporting

At its core, closed-loop reporting means closing the loop between the data that marketing is collecting—usually in a marketing automation system—and the data that the sales team is collecting which is generally seen in a CRM. If this is done properly, it allows marketers to make decisions on actions that occur further down the funnel based on what drives the greatest ROI for the business.

In my opinion, that is a limited definition and it is out of date because it does not consider the myriad of technologies that exist today for a marketer. Closing the loop for the modern marketer means that the data collected by all of the technologies can be tied back to each other to provide a complete view of the prospect. Typically, your CRM is the system that "closes the loop" between the various technologies but BI software is popular as well.

Let's look at what that means in detail in Figure 1. The diagram shows the various technologies supporting the different phases of the customer lifecycle. It also visually represents the closed-loop nicely. Each of the applications collects critical information relating to that stage. The data in these applications need to be combined into a central application for proper analysis.

A closer look at that diagram shows that two core technologies serve this function: the MAP and the CRM. The marketing automation tool is responsible for capturing all the data that is generated via marketing tactics. How much of that data is pushed into the CRM is up to the organization?

The CRM is responsible for capturing all mid-funnel to bottom-funnel data and allows the marketing activities in the MAP to be tracked to their ultimate disposition by either field sales, inside sales, or the BDR/SDR team

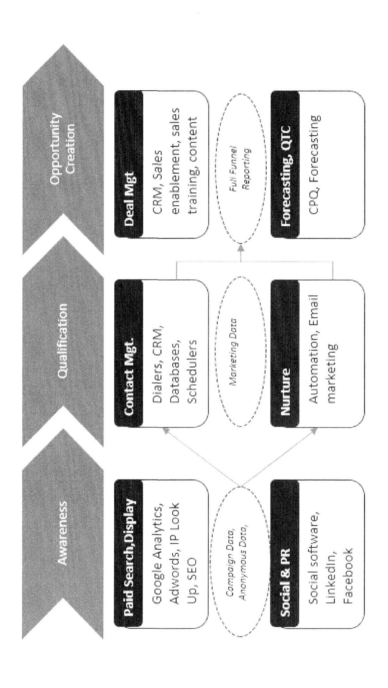

Figure 1 An example of a closed loop tech stack

In essence, closed-loop reporting allows the marketers to link their activities to people and then track them to their final disposition in the sales cycle. Without closed-loop reporting, your organization will have a difficult time measuring revenue impact.

Closed-loop reporting takes careful consideration of new technology and the integrations they support. Most companies choose to use their CRM as their source of truth but, as an organization grows, a BI tool becomes necessary to more easily ingest data from various sources.

Marketing Measurement Framework

The Marketing Measurement Framework (MMF) gives all stakeholders in the company visibility to the metrics that align with their job role and function, giving them confidence in their decision making and the ability to course-correct and improve marketing performance. It is a framework that guides you through the creation of actionable and audience-relevant dashboards while also laying a roadmap for future architecture and software.

An effective process will allow each stakeholder to express their core business objectives and then align reporting to measure their objectives. It will also uncover the technology, data, and process knowledge needed to create the proper reporting structure that is effective and confidence-inspiring.

The MMF is a three-step process that relies on three fundamental pillars that underly all effective reporting. The three pillars are data, technology and process, and audience.

Let's look at each one of these in more detail:

1. **Data**

    A dashboard is only as good as the data that underpins it. How do we ensure the data is correct? The best way to do that is to involve the stakeholders early in the process of data gathering. The stakeholders know their data better than anyone else and can often time spot errors in filters or errors in collection methodology. The goal is to have the stakeholders sign off on the data that will be used to create the dashboards. This is an important first step especially when you create dashboards for a new group.

2. **Technology and Process**

    These two are placed together because technology that is used without proper process will create poor data. Understanding which technologies collect the data you need is as critical as understanding the process by which that data is captured. When undergoing discovery during this step technology gaps and process breakdowns are often uncovered and will need to be fixed before proper data collection can begin. Sometimes it makes sense to collect the data that is available while understanding the gaps—while working to close those gaps with either a technology purchase or process improvement.

3. **Audience**

    It is also important to understand for whom the dashboard is being built. A marketing executive like the VP or CMO will not want some of the more tactical metrics that the PPC manager or webinar specialist will want. Again, the best way to accomplish that is to meet with the stakeholder and ask questions. What actions are they trying to drive? What questions are they seeking to answer? What are your key indicators of success?

With an understanding of the three foundational elements of the MMF, we can now look at the entire framework as seen in Figure 1. The first thing to understand is that it flows from the bottom to the top with the three foundational elements as the first items to understand.

The process begins with the first phase of strategy from which the key output is a draft of the reports and the dashboard to be created. The next step is the implementation in which the reports and dashboards are created within the technology decided upon in the earlier step. The final stage is an ongoing refinement and improvement of the reports as stakeholders become more comfortable digesting the data in its new form and they begin to learn more about their business through analysis.

You will also notice within each phase there are three core components: audience, objective, and output. Each phase must have the correct audience which is usually the people who are closest to the data and who understand the activities being captured. For instance, a CMO dashboard will have metrics the CMO is interested in but, to build the dashboard correctly, the operations department will need to meet with the people who are responsible for capturing the data in which the CMO is interested.

Strategy

Do not underestimate the amount of upfront work effective dashboarding will take. Without the proper discussions at the beginning with the correct stakeholders, dashboarding can wind up being siloed, improperly built, and therefore unused. To ensure that the right type of reporting is developed, first address the strategy which includes discovering the business requirements from the stakeholders, laying out the objectives, and then creating mock-ups of the dashboards and reports to be delivered.

Organizations that prioritize the strategy phase deliver measurement faster and more efficiently.

Audience

This step brings together the proper stakeholders to define the type of measurement that is being built. For example, is the initiative to build a CMO dashboard, evaluate function performance, or report on tactics?

Proper sponsorship is also an important part of the audience component. Measurement work that impacts multiple teams and requires participation from others within an organization will need the appropriate level of sponsorship to mobilize resources.

Objective

The objective of the key stakeholders in the strategy phase should be:

1. Information gathering activities to generate the information required to understand the data, the process for capturing the data, and the technologies responsible.

2. Uncovering data gaps that will allow you to identify process breakdowns, technology gaps, and/or technology implementation errors. The data gaps will be used in the final stage of improvement to drive future iterations of the dashboarding.

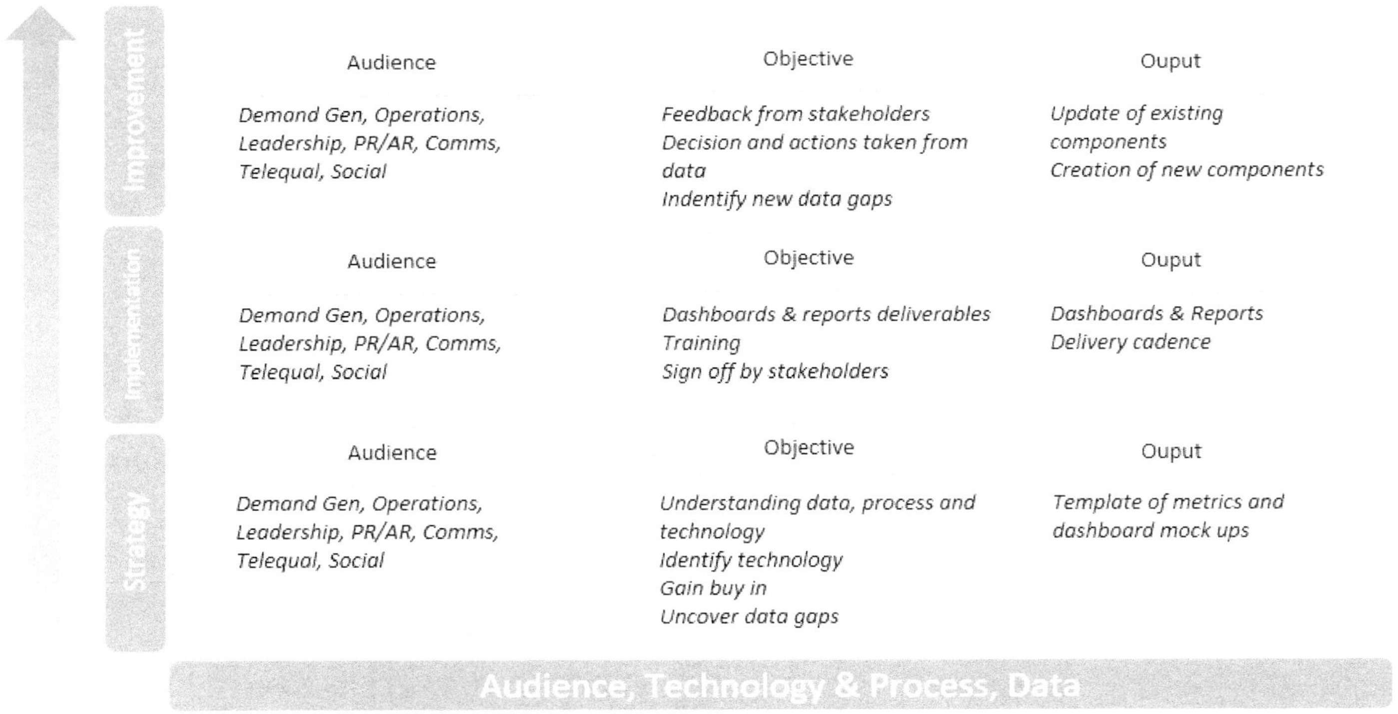

Audience, Technology & Process, Data

Strategy

- Audience: Demand Gen, Operations, Leadership, PR/AR, Comms, Telequal, Social
- Objective: Understanding data, process and technology; Identify technology; Gain buy in; Uncover data gaps
- Ouput: Template of metrics and dashboard mock ups

Implementation

- Audience: Demand Gen, Operations, Leadership, PR/AR, Comms, Telequal, Social
- Objective: Dashboards & reports deliverables; Training; Sign off by stakeholders
- Ouput: Dashboards & Reports; Delivery cadence

Improvement

- Audience: Demand Gen, Operations, Leadership, PR/AR, Comms, Telequal, Social
- Objective: Feedback from stakeholders; Decision and actions taken from data; Indentify new data gaps
- Ouput: Update of existing components; Creation of new components

Figure 1 The Marketing Measurement Framework

3. Finally, the stakeholders must gain buy-in from the sponsors and the members of the team on the understanding of the data, the process, and the technology.

Output

Once reporting needs are understood, the output stage translates those priorities into well-defined reporting deliverables:

1. A document with diagrams and a mock-up of reports and report types for the stakeholders to look at and edit. The document also outlines which technology will be used to deliver the reporting as well as the delivery cadence, e.g. on-demand, weekly, or monthly.
2. Among the most challenging aspects of the output stage is choosing the correct series of metrics that provide visibility into and express progress against the business objectives. Good dashboarding will have a selection of volume metrics that measure the quantity produced, such as the number of MQLs or SQLs, and efficiency metrics which measure how efficiently the produced quantity is being collected. Efficiency metrics often have a divisor of money and time. Cost per metrics are one of the most used efficiency metrics.

Implementation

The implementation phase focuses on taking the output of the strategy phase and creating working and usable reporting.

Audience

The audience in the implementation phase will most certainly include the members from the first phase but may also include a wider group like the CMO or executives who will receive the deliverables. For example, while the CMO might be part of the objective-setting within the strategy phase and be involved in setting the business requirements, they would not be involved in the data discovery process.

Objectives

The key objectives of the Implementation phase are:

1. For each defined reporting output, the list of included metrics and their definitions must be captured so future groups can track their origination and properly iterate them.

2. Delivery formats must be determined. Options typically include offline reporting with spreadsheets and presentation packages or online reporting with the business systems generating the data.

3. Layout and visualization of the data is a priority so that it is easily digestible, tells the correct story, and can be actioned upon. Charts must depict meaningful comparisons and make it easy for audiences to make sense of the information.

4. Training is one of the most often overlooked objectives of the implementation phase and the one that causes reporting to fail. Training plans must be completed to

ensure the reporting is well understood so it can be used in decision-making.

Output

The output of the implementation phase is the delivery of the reporting and dashboards to the appropriate stakeholders.

Improvement

The Improvement phase assesses whether the reporting is helping to meet the business challenges identified. That phase can bring forward the data and technology gaps you learned of in the strategy phase.

Audience

The audience in the Improvement stage is the stakeholders digesting the information and using it to make business decisions.

Objectives

The objectives of this phase are:

1. Reporting that is not used cannot create positive change. Try to understand whether the reporting is being used for decision-making and how effective those decisions were in driving the expected behavior.

2. Solicit feedback from users to understand how well the reporting is meeting their needs.

3. Discover what data is missing or you are unable to capture due to missing technology, bad process, or incorrect data structures.

Output

The main output at this stage is a roadmap for continuous structured improvement. A good roadmap will contain the following two items.

The first is a list of reporting improvements and enhancements that will allow the organization to mature its reporting needs in a manner consistent with its business objectives. The roadmap is a living document that tracks updates to existing reporting and the initiation of new reporting efforts.

The second is a list of the data that is not currently available due to the reasons mentioned above in the objectives section. Missing data is often caused by missing or poorly implemented technology, bad processes. and/or poorly constructed data architecture. Understanding which of these three elements is the root cause of your missing data is important to solving the problem. In my experience, data is the main culprit for bad reporting and many companies struggle to keep their data clean. To help, I have listed some examples of each of these issues in the table below:

Symptom	Root Cause	Solution
Campaign attribution missing from leads in CRM	MAP system is poorly implemented	Confirm campaign objects are properly synced between MAP and CRM

Unable to track campaign effectiveness down to the tactical level	Poorly implemented campaign architecture	Read Chapter II to understand a properly implemented data architecture for your campaigns
Missing/Incomplete data from list loads	A bad list load process	Document the list load process

Figure 2 Table of common issues that often occur with data loading

Understanding and embracing the framework will help you support your organization to meet its business objectives by providing reporting that is useful, accurate, and constantly improving. Ultimately, good reporting positions MO as a critical piece of an organization's strategy. Further, it gives the individual members of the team a thorough understanding of the business drivers of the organization, positioning them as indispensable employees.

Marketing Operations Reporting

Until now, we have only talked about dashboarding that helps an organization meet its strategic goals within the MMF. However, the marketing operations can also benefit from the MMF to help govern their department and strive toward continuous improvement. All the principles of the MMF apply to the marketing operations department.

The focus is on the improvement and the maturity of the analytics they can capture to help them become a more valuable operations department. The ticketing system will contain a lot of that information for how well tickets are being handled and how satisfied the marketing department is with the service the operations team is providing.

Reports focused on data completeness, cleanliness and accuracy are also valuable to understand how well the marketing operations department is governing their data collection.

7
The Future of Marketing Operations

A Look Back

Over my twenty years in marketing operations, I have seen the discipline grow to become a critical part of an organization's marketing strategy. The CMO now looks to the department to help set a budget, allocate campaign spending, predict bookings based upon a tactical mix, and guide decisions throughout the year. A strong marketing operations organization can make or break a marketing department's success.

Figure 1 shows the shift in importance the organization has taken regarding the charter, staffing, funding, and technology investment.

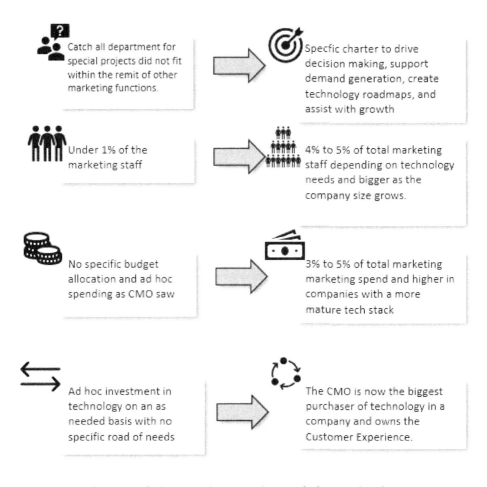

Figure 1 Marketing operations maturity over the last two decades

Moving Beyond Marketing

Customers reward strong brands with repeat purchases, advocacy, and loyalty. Capturing and keeping the customer has never been more important in a digital age where information is at the consumer's fingertips and there are relatively few barriers to switching.

Well-informed customers will want to do business with companies that know them and their business intimately. Customers will expect a personalized experience. They will expect companies to know their business inside and out and use their knowledge to design products and services that create a frictionless experience. To do that, companies must:

1. Engage in a collaborative, consultative relationship with customers starting with the very first interaction they have via the website, social site, or downloaded content.

2. Capture more information, including how the company operates and its growth plans.

3. Know more about the individual interests and personalities of those involved on the purchasing committee.

To accomplish the items above, an organization must break down data silos between departments because often these data points reside in several different departments. An organization must be able to share data across technology platforms and departments to build one view of the truth from which each department can make reliable customer-driven decisions.

A coordinated and cohesive customer experience strategy is critical for consistent revenue growth. Historically, there have been two departments that manage the operations of the customer experience. Marketing operations are responsible for branding, messaging, first impressions, and top-of-the-funnel activities. Sales operations is responsible for creating customers and then keeping those customers with their customer success organization.

Having two different departments service the two main groups who provide customer experience inhibits collaboration and creates data silos. Often, these two groups are buying overlapping technology, creating conflicting processes, and distributing data that only tells half of the story. Forward-thinking executives are looking for a better way to manage the operations of these two groups to improve customer experience and create consistent revenue growth. Consider these statistics on the importance of aligning the two functions:

1. 85 percent of sales and marketing alignment is the largest opportunity for improving business performance today.[15]

2. 96 percent of sales and marketing executives agree that marketing and sales don't measure success on the same KPIs and don't share goals and objectives.[16]

3. Companies with aligned revenue engines grow 19 percent faster and are 15 percent more profitable.[17]

---

[15] https://business.linkedin.com/content/dam/me/business/en-us/marketing-solutions/cx/2020/images/pdfs/moments-of-trust-v4.pdf?__hstc=82794953.d67d763751a44186dd77eb200afc3643.1609517790121.160951779012 1.1609517790121.1&__hssc=82794953.1.1609517790122&__hsfp=1332846724
[16] https://business.linkedin.com/content/dam/me/business/en-us/marketing-solutions/cx/2020/images/pdfs/moments-of-trust-v4.pdf?__hstc=82794953.d67d763751a44186dd77eb200afc3643.1609517790121.160951779012 1.1609517790121.1&__hssc=82794953.1.1609517790122&__hsfp=1332846724
[17] https://www.pardot.com/blog/5-key-takeaways-from-siriusdecisions-summit-19/

Rise of Revenue Operations

This emerging go-to-market structure—which brings the operations teams supporting sales, marketing, and customer success together under one umbrella—is called revenue operations. Revenue operations integrates and aligns the operational functions that power the revenue engine into one strategic team focused on maximizing an organization's growth and performance across the entire revenue chain.

Revenue operations (RevOps) delivers a focus on aligning sales, marketing, and customer success across the entire customer journey. RevOps attempts to break the traditionally siloed marketing, sales, and customer success data and strategies to create a more consistent approach across an organization. Successful teams align the revenue engine to maximize an organization's growth and create a customer experience that gives them a competitive advantage. They accomplish that with a focus on collecting, sharing, and utilizing data effectively to harness actionable insights and make effective data-backed decisions.

The main objectives of a RevOps team are to:

✓ **Create alignment** Align marketing, sales, support, and success teams around common goals.

✓ **Facilitate focus** Bring teams together around common success metrics and align the organization on one view of the truth.

✓ **Simplify** RevOps teams often strive to simplify business processes and strategies to make them easier to manage and execute. Simplification often comes with the consolidation of technology, as well.

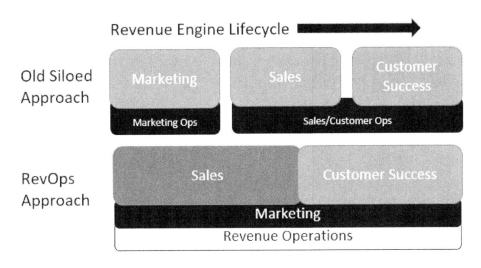

Figure 2 RevOps approach to supporting the revenue engine

Growth of Revenue Operations

Revenue operations is not a trend that is likely to fade over time. Public companies that adopt revenue operations realize 71 percent higher stock growth over their competitors who do not embrace the revenue operations model.[18] Revenue operations titles have significantly outpaced other operations titles in recent years. Chief Revenue Officer roles only slightly outpaced Chief Sales Officer titles but Director Revenue Operations surpasses Director of Sales Operations titles by a whopping 68 percent.[19]

---

[18] https://go.forrester.com/blogs/revenue-operations-and-cmos/
[19] https://www.clari.com/blog/the-rise-of-revenue-operations-infographic

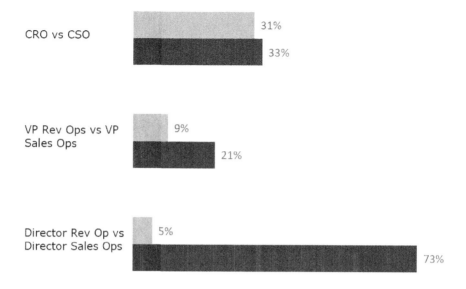

CRO vs CSO   31%
              33%

VP Rev Ops vs VP   9%
Sales Ops   21%

Director Rev Op vs   5%
Director Sales Ops   73%

Figure 3 Courtesy of Clari @ https://www.clari.com/blog/the-rise-of-revenue-operations-infographic

Future of Marketing Operations

The need for excellent marketing operations talent is at an all-time high. Salaries rise into the six digits with five years' experience and companies are recruiting heavily. The CMO is under immense pressure to track and prove ROI. A recent study that tracked the C-suite movement of the 100 most advertised brands in the country found that: [20]

---

[20]https://www.morningbrew.com/marketing/stories/2021/04/30/cmo-tenure-hits-new-low

1. Average CMO tenure dropped to forty months in 2020, down from forty-one in 2019.

2. Median tenure fell to twenty-five and a half months, the lowest ever recorded, from thirty months in 2019.

3. The average CEO tenure is about six and a half years for comparison.

With such a short tenure and heavy reliance on technology and reporting, the CMO relies on the marketing operations organization for a myriad of strategic tasks.

Effective marketing campaigns use data to properly segment the audience and craft the message. Once created, the message must be efficiently delivered to the target audience which requires different technologies depending on the tactic. Both of those critical tasks by the CMO require the operations department to succeed.

The future of marketing operations is bright. Technologies that assist the CMO in targeting audiences, delivering the message, and gaining customer insight will always be required. Without a talented operations team, the CMO cannot be agile enough to adapt to new marketing challenges. To put it bluntly, the marketing operations team is the engine behind the CMO's strategy.

In working with many CMOs, I see a pattern. CMOs who try to tackle challenges with a suboptimal marketing operations organization tend to fail. Those who tackle their challenges with a strong marketing operations team succeed.